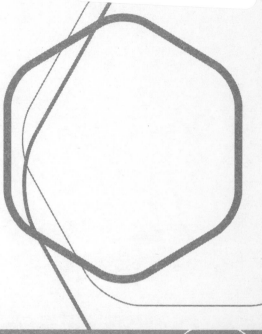

Succeed at psychometric testing

PRACTICE TESTS FOR
DIAGRAMMATIC
& ABSTRACT REASONING

New edition

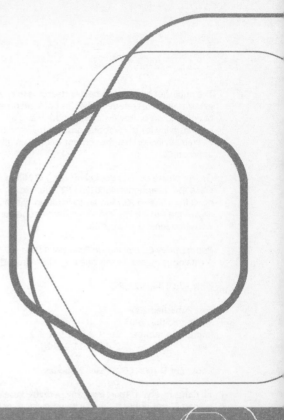

Succeed at psychometric testing

PRACTICE TESTS FOR
DIAGRAMMATIC
& ABSTRACT REASONING

HODDER
EDUCATION
PART OF HACHETTE LIVRE UK

Peter S. Rhodes

New edition

Orders: please contact Bookpoint Ltd, 130 Milton Park, Abingdon, Oxon OX14 4SB. Telephone: (44) 01235 827720. Fax: (44) 01235 400454. Lines are open from 9.00–5.00, Monday to Saturday, with a 24-hour message answering service. You can also order through our website www.hoddereducation.co.uk.

British Library Cataloguing in Publication Data
A catalogue record for this title is available from the British Library.

ISBN: 978 0 340 97228 1

First Published 2004
Second edition 2008
Impression number   10 9 8 7 6 5 4 3 2
Year   2012 2011 2010

Typeset by Servis Filmsetting Ltd, Stockport, Cheshire.
Printed in Great Britain for Hodder Education, an Hachette Livre UK Company, 338 Euston Road, London NW1 3BH by CPI Cox & Wyman, Reading, Berkshire, RG1 8EX.

Hachette Livre UK's policy is to use papers that are natural, renewable and recyclable products and made from wood grown in sustainable forests. The logging and manufacturing processes are expected to conform to the environmental regulations of the country of origin.

CONTENTS

ACKNOWLEDGEMENTS

I would like to thank Sarah McAfee for her assistance in the preparation of the test items. I would also like to thank colleagues at OTL, particularly Valerie Newton and Richard Littledale for their forbearance once again while I took time out to produce another book.

Acknowledgement is also made to:

- ASE, London, UK
- The Psychological Corporation, Texas
- Oxford Psychologists Press, UK
- SHL, London, UK.

FOREWORD

Should anyone tell you that a psychometric test will give an accurate indication of your level of intelligence, don't pay too much attention. It isn't necessarily true.

The credibility of the global psychometric testing industry rests on the belief of employers that a psychometric test will yield accurate and reliable data about a candidate's ability. Busy employers buy into the notion that a psychometric test will swiftly eliminate all the unsuitable candidates and deliver up only the best, brightest and most able candidates to the interview stage.

What is not widely known is that it is perfectly possibly for a candidate to drastically improve their own psychometric score by adopting a methodical approach to test preparation. The purpose of the *Succeed at Psychometric Testing* series is to provide you with the necessary tools for this purpose.

It is useful to know that a candidate's ability to perform well in a psychometric test is determined by a wide range of factors, aside from the difficulty of the questions in the test. External factors include the test environment and the professionalism of the test administrator; internal factors relate to the candidate's confidence level on the day, the amount of previous test practice the candidate has and the candidate's self-belief that they will succeed. While you cannot always control the external factors, you can manage many of the internal factors.

A common complaint from test takers is the lack of practice material available to them. The titles in the *Succeed at Psychometric Testing* series address this gap and the series is designed with you, the test taker in mind. The content focuses on practice and explanations rather than on the theory and science. The authors are all experienced test takers and understand the benefits of thorough test preparation. They have prepared the content with the test taker's priorities in mind. Research has shown us that test takers don't have much notice of their test, so they need lots of practice, right now, in an environment that simulates the real test as closely as possible.

In all the research for this series, I have met only one person who likes – or rather, doesn't mind – taking psychometric tests. This person is a highly successful and senior manager in the NHS and she has taken psychometric tests for many of the promotions for which she has applied. Her attitude to the process is sanguine: 'I have to do it, I can't get out of it and I want the promotion so I might as well get on with it.' She always does well. A positive mental attitude is absolutely crucial in preparing yourself for your upcoming test and will undoubtedly help you on the day. If you spend time practising beforehand and become familiar with the format of the test, you are already in charge of some of the factors that deter other candidates on the day.

It's worth bearing in mind that the skills you develop in test preparation will be useful to you in your everyday life and in your new job. For many people, test preparation is not the most joyful way to spend free time, but know that by doing so, you are not wasting your time.

The *Succeed at Psychometric Testing* series covers the whole spectrum of skills and tests presented by the major test publishers and will help you prepare for your numerical, verbal, logical, abstract and diagrammatic reasoning tests. The series now also includes a title on personality testing. This new title will help you understand the role that personality testing plays in both the recruitment process and explains how such tests can also help you to identify areas of work to which you, personally, are most suited. The structure of each title is designed to help you to mark your practice tests quickly and find an expert's explanation to the questions you have found difficult.

If you don't attain your best score at your first attempt, don't give up. Book yourself in to retake the test in a couple of months, go away and practise the tests again. Psychometric scores are not absolute and with practice, you can improve your score.

Good luck! Let us know how you get on.

Heidi Smith, Series Editor
educationenquiries@hodder.co.uk

Other titles in the series:

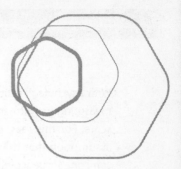

CHAPTER ONE
INTRODUCTION

WHY READ THIS BOOK?

It arrives. The job advert could have been written with you in mind. You applied and now are through to the next stage. The letter informs you that as well as the interview there is going to be a psychometric test. Your heart sinks. And you are starting to worry. You have not taken a test before or have not done one for years. Or worse still, the last time you took a test you were told you had not done very well.

But one of the best-kept secrets about psychological tests is that it is possible to improve your score dramatically.

Psychologists who devise tests and test publishers who publish them do not talk about this much. Publishers' test sales depend on their clients' having faith in the value of testing. They encourage organisations who purchase their materials to think that measuring aspects of someone's ability is as straightforward as measuring their height or weight. But it is not. For example, if you were to measure your height today and tomorrow, next month, or in two months' time you will get the same result. But if you were to take psychometric tests on different occasions it is almost certain that you will not get the same result.

With psychological tests, scores change. This is because unlike measuring height a lot of factors go into producing your test score. For this reason, psychometric tests are based on the assumption that they give only a glimpse or an estimate of someone's 'true score'. Traditional psychometric theory suggests a person's score on any test is made up of his or her 'true score', i.e. real level of ability, and 'junk'. Junk is all the factors (such as anxiety, low expectations of success, lack of confidence, confusing directions) which get in the way of your being able to do your best.

Unfortunately, the idea that a test score is essentially a 'sample' providing at best a probabilistic estimate of someone's ability is very often forgotten in organisational test usage. And often test scores are treated as if they are straightforwardly 'true', with little account taken of the degree of error they may contain.

With this in mind this book is partly about ensuring that when you come to take the test there is, for you, no 'junk'; there is nothing getting in the way of your being able to do yourself justice on the test. But the aim of this book goes beyond this relatively modest goal. Whilst traditional psychometric theory assumes there is a 'true score', some psychologists would argue there is no such thing, no true score, no relatively fixed level of ability established by a psychometric test. What they would argue is that ability tests essentially measure discrete 'task skills' (i.e. the ability to do specific tasks) rather than the more fundamental and fixed human capacities which test publishers claim they measure. And task skills are, by definition, much more malleable. The view this book will adopt, therefore, is that diagrammatic/abstract reasoning tests involve task skills which can easily be developed.

This book therefore is about enabling you to improve your score on diagrammatic/abstract reasoning tests by:

- removing some of the well documented factors likely to reduce your performance
- coaching you on the task skills involved in diagrammatic/ abstract reasoning tests.

SO HOW CAN I IMPROVE MY SCORE?

There is a great deal of research evidence to suggest that, unlike measuring height or weight, scores on psychometric tests of ability are affected by a number of factors. There are at least five factors which this book can help you with.

EXPECTATION OF SUCCESS

There is a vast body of research demonstrating that one of the crucial determinants of your test performance is the extent to which you feel you are likely to do well.

This book is not intended as an academic text and so detailed review of this evidence is not appropriate, so to illustrate the importance of the expectation of success just one study will suffice here. In this carefully conducted study (reported in one of the more reputable academic journals), individuals were divided into two groups. Each group was required to do the same ability test. The only difference was that one group was given instructions which suggested they may find the test difficult. The other group was told they would find the test interesting and challenging. The hormone levels of individuals in each group were carefully monitored.

Even though the instructions differed by only a few words, the two groups appeared to go down completely different biochemical pathways. The 'interesting challenge' group filled up with hormones making it easier for them to focus their attention on the test. The 'difficult challenge' group went down a biochemical pathway which meant their blood streams filled up with hormones making them anxious and this made it more difficult for them to focus their attention effectively.

This study vividly illustrates the importance of expectations. How you feel about the test appears to have a profound physio-logical effect. If you feel confident and prepared, you are more likely to go down a biochemical pathway that helps you focus than if you feel the test is likely to be difficult and challenging.

So, use this book to ensure you feel ready and prepared for the demands of the task. Do the practice tests and then if necessary do them again and again until you feel you are prepared.

TEST SOPHISTICATION

Another well established factor, likely to affect your performance, is your level of familiarity with tests. This was a big issue in the UK when the 11+ exam was compulsory. The outcome of the 11+ could affect the rest of a child's life. And so, not surprisingly, a cottage industry of teachers coaching the children of anxious parents grew up. There was evidence at the time that this coaching had a significant effect on performance in the exam. I have further more recent anecdotal evidence of the impact of coaching. A colleague coached his daughter on the diagrammatic/abstract reasoning tests used in the 11+. The county he lived in had retained the selective system and the 11+ was used to determine which children would be offered places at the local grammar schools. His daughter's initial performance placed her well outside the top 25 per cent required to secure a place. After several attempts on different tests and coaching on the rationales of typical questions, his daughter's performance steadily improved. She won her place at the grammar school.

For some time, test publishers have encouraged their clients to send out 'practice sets'. This was largely as a result of pressure from the Commission for Racial Equality who felt that for some minority groups the experience of being tested was extremely alien and that often the example questions publishers normally included in their test booklets were not comprehensive enough to bring everyone up to an even playing field.

It may well be that you have already received yours or will receive a set in due course. These sets usually provide a very small number of practice questions, yet the evidence suggests the more coaching the better. So in addition to the materials you receive from the publisher, the practice items available to you in this book will help you improve your performance even more.

SPEED

Related to both these issues is the fundamental one of your *response strategy* during the test. Some people prefer accuracy to speed, others will trade some accuracy for getting through more questions. Generally, accuracy is not really taken into account when interpreting your test performance in organisational settings. This would take test interpretation into a much more 'qualitative' area similar to that employed in educational and clinical settings where thinking style and how someone coped with the materials – for example, how frustrated someone seemed – are as important as what score was achieved.

In organisational usage, interpreting test performance is more straightforward. The issue is simply how many you got right compared with some relevant comparison group.

This means three golden rules apply:

- Always trade off accuracy for speed (although not to the point where you are not paying sufficient attention to questions).
- Always do as many questions as possible.
- Never spend too much time on any one question.

The higher your expectation of success and your familiarity with test items, the more items you are likely to be able to attempt. Speed is important in most tests but it is particularly important in diagrammatic/abstract reasoning tests.

One reason for this is the way in which tests are scored and interpreted. One of the sad realities of life is that most of us are average. And this means virtually all tests have the same distribution of test scores (see Figure 1.1). Most scores bunch up around some average point. It is of course the same with height, weight or shoe size. The fact that we all tend to have roughly the same size feet, with only a relatively small number of individuals having extremely big or small feet, makes

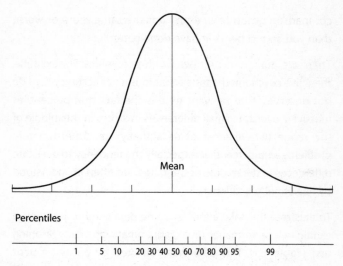

Figure 1.1 The Normal Distribution and percentiles

stocking shoes easier: more shoes of an average size will be required.

This characteristic distribution of scores has very profound implications which you are able to take advantage of. What the 'hump' in the middle means, as suggested, is that most scores tend to bunch up around a middle point. Now the statistic which most organisations in the UK use to interpret test performance is the *percentile*.

This statistic is not to be confused with a percentage. If you are not familiar with the term it refers to the proportion of a comparison group who would get the same score (or a worse score) than you. This sounds like an odd definition. But it means you are on the 65 percentile if 65 per cent of people in the comparison group have either got the same score or worse than you and 35 per cent have done better.

There are numerous problems with percentiles. For example, they give psychometric tests a spurious air of accuracy they do not deserve. More relevant here is the fact that percentiles massively overstate small differences in scores in the middle of the range (where most of us actually are). Unfortunately, problems with percentiles, especially the tendency to overstate differences in the middle of the range, are often ill-understood by Personnel practitioners.

To illustrate this take a look at some data used to interpret a candidate's performance on a diagrammatic/abstract reasoning test (Table 1.1). This data was collected by an assessment consultancy, OTL, but is similar to that provided by test publishers to organisations used to assess the performance of candidates.

In this typical data, only ten scores separate those on the 75th percentile from those on the 25th. The test has 40 questions. As percentiles understate differences at the extremes there is only a two percentile difference between those who get 33 and those who get 40 (97th and 99th percentiles). So all the 'action' in percentile terms is in the middle range. If you think about this, if you are in the centre of the range (which is where most of us are), it needs only a slight improvement to shift your score, *in percentile terms*, quite dramatically. For example, only four more questions attempted and answered correctly could take you from the 40th to the 60th percentile on this particular diagrammatic/abstract reasoning test. Some norms produce even more dramatic increments than this. The more the score is interpreted against a 'restricted group', such as

Table 1.1

Candidate's score	Percentile
26	75
25	70
24	65
23	60
22	55
21	50
20	45
19	40
18	35
17	30
16	25

managers or supervisors, the more pronounced this effect is likely to be.

The reality is that these relatively insignificant differences in scores tend to be over-interpreted in organisational settings. A selection panel would assume the candidate on the 60th percentile is significantly better than the one who is 'only' on the 40th percentile. But the difference could be the result of one candidate making two lucky guesses and somebody else having two unlucky guesses.

The key point here is *that for most of us a small shift in response rate can have a significant impact on the percentile we achieve.*

So the more practice you have the more confidence you will develop and the more rapidly you will be able to progress through any set of questions.

INTERPRETATION OF THE TASK

Another key determinant of your score is your understanding of what is required of you by the test. At a basic level, this means ensuring you understand where the answer block is (yes people do sometimes fill in the wrong block on sheets which contain answer blocks for more than one test). It also means ensuring you are clear how you are supposed to fill in the answer sheet and what are the correct responses: whether you are supposed to be filling in circles, underlining, crossing out or ticking.

At a more complex level, *interpretation of the task*, is about the extent to which you have been 'psychologically engaged' by the complexity of the exercise and understand exactly how the test works – what the 'rules' are. This book helps here because all three of the major item styles for diagrammatic/abstract reasoning tests are described and explained.

If however the employer is using a test from an obscure source which this book does not simulate then it is important to ensure the test administrator does his or her job effectively. If you do not understand why you have got an example wrong or indeed if you have got an example correct but are not 100 per cent certain why it is the correct answer then say. There is no shame or embarrassment attached to getting examples wrong or seeking clarification. In fact, a good administrator ought to create an environment where you are encouraged to ask questions.

THE ENVIRONMENT

Environmental factors have a huge impact on your performance. It is important you are tested in a room with adequate heating, ventilation, lighting and free from interruptions. Whilst this might seem obvious, I have encountered organisations who test in public areas such as reception and corridors or use a manager's office where the manager may be away for the day – but whose phone keeps ringing.

Unlike your familiarity with tests and your expectation of success, you have less immediate control over this area. The quality of the environment is the test administrator's responsibility. If he or she has been properly trained and is aware of the responsibility to create an environment which is, for example, free from distraction, then they ought to act in order to minimise any distractions which occur.

Do not be afraid to complain and point out any deficiencies in testing conditions. Most test publishers produce a 'test log' and include it with the answer sheets. This encourages test administrators to note anything which might affect your test performance. What is in the test log should be taken into account when interpreting your performance.

WHAT IS DIAGRAMMATIC/ABSTRACT REASONING?

This might surprise you but diagrammatic/abstract reasoning tests are based on an idea which appeared at the turn of the last century. This is the idea that *intelligence is one thing*. This idea has been in and out of fashion over the last hundred years. Currently, it is very much back in fashion.

The idea was first suggested by Charles Spearman, a psychologist who spent half his life in the psychological laboratory and the other half on the battlefield. As well as making an enduring contribution to psychology, he was also a senior military figure who was decorated three times. It might seem astonishing to think Spearman's influence on modern psychology and particularly contemporary psychometric tests continues to be as strong now as it was at the beginning of the last century. You may think this reflects poorly on psychology as a science. How can research from the beginning of the last century still influence current thinking? The answer lies in the robustness of Spearman's original research and conclusions.

Spearman defined intelligence as the 'innate ability to perceive relationships and educe co-relationships'. Educe is not a word we use much nowadays. The root word of educate, it essentially means 'to draw out'. Diagrammatic/abstract reasoning tests involve doing precisely this – identifying relationships and establishing what follows.

What Spearman discovered was that people's performance on different kinds of ability test seems to be highly consistent. In other words, people who do well, for example on a test of numerical reasoning also do well on tests of verbal reasoning. This led Spearman to suggest that intelligence is one 'thing'.

This went against the wisdom of the time which believed in 'faculties' which were independent of each other. People were considered to have a 'profile' of faculties such as judgement, memory, invention and attention. The largest employer in the world at the time, a railway company, had huge numbers of staff assessed and elaborate profiles drawn up of nine separate 'faculties'. (These included, amongst others, concentration, observation, quick grasp, and distractibility.)

Spearman's influence on psychology and psychological testing has been enormous. In fact, this book is a testament to his continued influence as diagrammatic/abstract reasoning tests are seen as coming closest to measuring his idea of 'eductive power'. So all of the practice tests in this book flow straight-forwardly from his 1904 definition of intelligence – perceiving relationships and working out what follows. And whilst there has been renewed interest recently in the idea of 'multiple intelligences' and an attempt to return to an idea of relatively independent faculties, these ideas have not had much impact on psychometric tests in the UK.

Diagrammatic/abstract reasoning tests are often referred to as tests of intelligence. In fact, strictly speaking, they are not. They only measure certain aspects of mental functioning. But tests of diagrammatic/abstract reasoning, although never originally intended to be used *on their own* as measures of general intelligence, are very often used in this way in organisations. The argument for using them in this way is that they seem to represent the best single measure of general intelligence available. So, if intelligence is one thing, it is also seen as bucket shaped – with some of us having bigger buckets than others. And the quickest way of finding out how big our buckets are is to use a diagrammatic/abstract reasoning test.

WHY AM I BEING ASKED TO DO A DIAGRAMMATIC/ABSTRACT REASONING TEST?

The discussion above has described how the prevailing view of intelligence is that it is one thing and the best single estimate of it is performance on a diagrammatic/abstract reasoning test. This view has a number of implications for psychometric testing in organisations and society more generally.

For example, Spearman's idea that intelligence is one thing implies that elaborate assessment processes involving measurement of a number of supposedly separate abilities is to a large extent a waste of time. Yes, there may well be some differences, for example between your scores on a numerical reasoning and on a verbal reasoning test, but Spearman's argument would be that this may well be due to chance factors – junk – rather than because they tell us anything more interesting and important about your ability structure.

Therefore, for Spearman, running a number of tests with candidates means measuring general intelligence over and over with different amounts of 'junk' caused in each test because, for example, there may be specific linguistic demands or issues of exposure to numerical technique that a test involves but these represent 'noise' which gets in the way of estimating intelligence.

The argument for the use of diagrammatic/abstract reasoning tests is that they provide most of the predictive power of ability tests in occupational settings. In the workplace, measures of general intelligence, as assessed by diagrammatic/abstract reasoning tests account for somewhere between 10 and 25 per cent of the differences in our effectiveness in job roles. Whether it is nearer 25 per cent depends on the nature of the job. The more the job involves grasping the essentials of complex issues and thinking in a logical and orderly way in order to identify potential solutions the more performance on the test is likely to be predictive of effectiveness in the role.

You may be asked to do a diagrammatic/abstract reasoning test because it provides a useful check on other scores (it is the least 'contaminated' by education).

In addition, whilst these are not unrelated factors, the rationale for using diagrammatic/abstract reasoning tests should be because the role you are applying for involves:

- coping with a high degree of novelty
- coping with a high level of complexity
- performing non-routine/non-programmatic tasks where there is no 'custom and practice' to fall back on
- having to think on your feet (adapting quickly to what is new and changing in the environment)
- having to absorb prodigious amounts of information quickly
- identifying trends, relationships and patterns in data
- policy/strategy formulation (seeing issues at different levels of analysis)
- research and development
- information technology (all programming aptitude tests are essentially tests of general intelligence).

If the job you are applying for involves using well delineated systems, policies and procedures or using the skills, experiences and insights which you have already developed, then a diagrammatic/abstract reasoning test is of little value in indicating how you will cope. This means the test administrator will struggle to explain to you why you are being asked to complete the test.

There is also the possibility that the use of the diagrammatic/ abstract reasoning test simply reflects a common corporate orthodoxy – 'a bright hire is a smart hire'. In other words, the belief in the organisation may simply be that it is better to have 'brighter' people selected even though there may be no evidence for the effectiveness of the test at predicting genuine differences in work performance. One of the reasons for the spectacular downfall of Enron in 2002 was that it was obsessed with hiring very bright young people and allowing them to move into markets and countries they knew nothing about. The assumption was they would succeed because they were bright. In the event, the disastrous deals they did and the subsequent losses they created crippled the company. As Enron employees who lost their jobs and shareholders who had their pensions and savings invested in the company know to their cost, simply being smart is often not enough to guarantee success in a role.

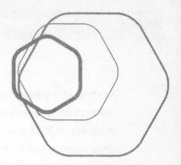

CHAPTER TWO
TIMED TESTS

Much of the value of this book is that it provides you with opportunities to practise test questions which simulate those you are likely to encounter in a selection setting.

There are currently over 50 test publishers in the UK. These range from 'one-man bands' selling materials from residential addresses, through to offshoots of large corporate entities. Assessment for Selection and Employment (ASE) for example is a subsidiary of Granada (you may think *Coronation Street* and psychological tests seem like odd bedfellows).

The goal of this book is to provide you with the maximum probability of success. The practice tests that follow have been designed to simulate the materials from the four largest test publishers – ASE, The Psychological Corporation, Oxford Psychologists Press and SHL.

There are however only four tests. This is because two of the publishers have similar item styles. The SHL diagrammatic tests are direct descendants of the abstract reasoning element of the Differential Aptitude Test (DAT), originally published in 1947 by the Psychological Corporation. The Differential Aptitude Test has a new edition and so may well be encountered in a selection context.

In short, this book covers the main possibilities. And even if you were to be given something from a more obscure source or even something which had been developed internally by the organisation, it is likely to resemble one of the three main item styles.

TEST 1: SHL/DAT ITEM STYLE

(Answers to this test may be found on pages 131–138.)

Get a piece of paper and find a place where you have adequate space to write on and are not likely to be interrupted.

You will also need a stopwatch or a watch with a timer.

Read through the example questions. Make sure you are clear what is expected by the question format. Each question has a set of problem figures followed by a set of answer figures. The task is to establish which of the answer figures would be the next one, or the fifth, in the series of problem figures.

When you are ready to begin, start your stopwatch or watch.

EXAMPLE 1

PROBLEM FIGURE

ANSWER FIGURE

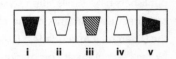

i ii iii iv v

The Problem Figures alternate between displaying a black trapezium and a white trapezium. As the last Problem Figure has a black trapezium, the next figure in the series will be a white trapezium. The correct Answer Figure for this example is therefore **Figure ii**.

EXAMPLE 2

PROBLEM FIGURE

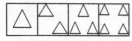

ANSWER FIGURE

One extra triangle is added to each new Problem Figure. As the last Problem Figure has four triangles, the next figure in the series will have five triangles. The correct Answer Figure for this example is therefore **Figure v**.

TEST 1

You have 20 minutes to complete this test.

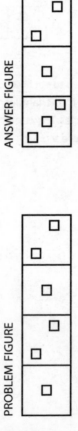

PROBLEM FIGURE

ANSWER FIGURE

a   b   c   d   e

2

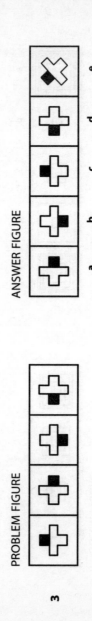

PROBLEM FIGURE

3

ANSWER FIGURE

a   b   c   d   e

4

PROBLEM FIGURE

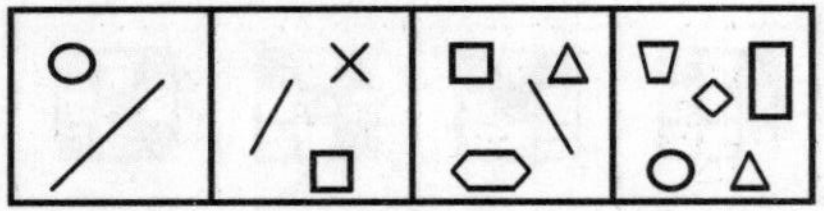

ANSWER FIGURE

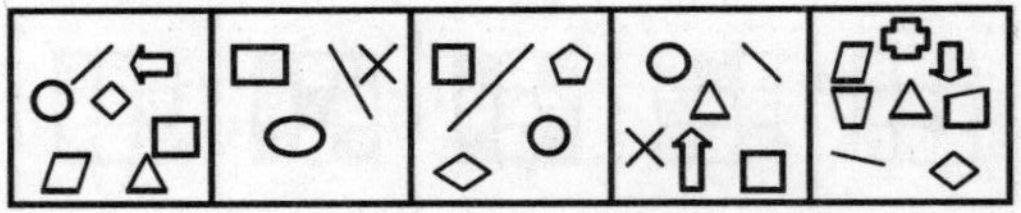

a   b   c   d   e

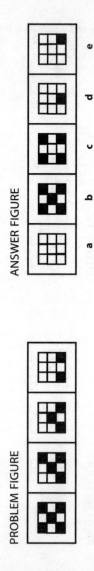

ANSWER FIGURE

a   b   c   d   e

PROBLEM FIGURE

5

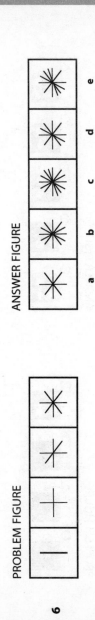

ANSWER FIGURE

a   b   c   d   e

PROBLEM FIGURE

6

PROBLEM FIGURE

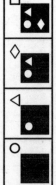

7

ANSWER FIGURE

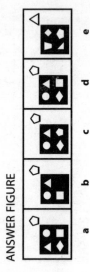

a   b   c   d   e

PROBLEM FIGURE

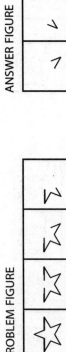

8

ANSWER FIGURE

a   b   c   d   e

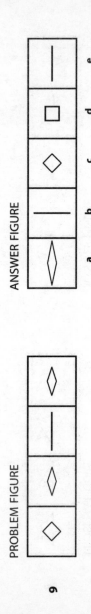

ANSWER FIGURE

PROBLEM FIGURE

9

28

PROBLEM FIGURE

10

ANSWER FIGURE

a   b   c   d   e

ANSWER FIGURE

PROBLEM FIGURE

11

12

PROBLEM FIGURE

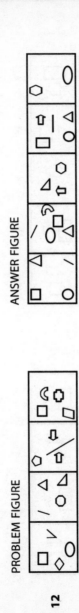

ANSWER FIGURE

a b c d e

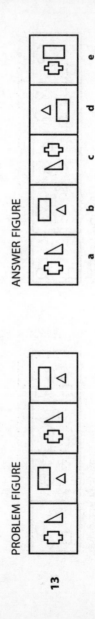

ANSWER FIGURE

PROBLEM FIGURE

13

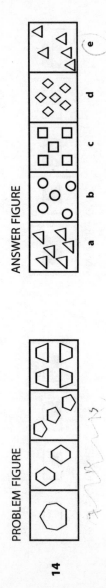

PROBLEM FIGURE

ANSWER FIGURE

14

a   b   c   d   e

33

PROBLEM FIGURE

ANSWER FIGURE

a   b   c   d   e

15

PROBLEM FIGURE

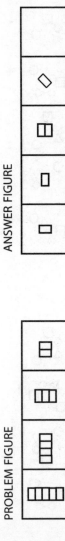

16

ANSWER FIGURE

a   b   c   d   e

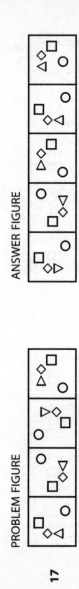

PROBLEM FIGURE

ANSWER FIGURE

a b c d e

17

PROBLEM FIGURE

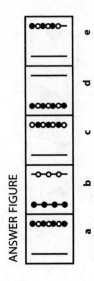

ANSWER FIGURE

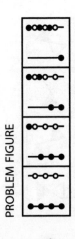

18

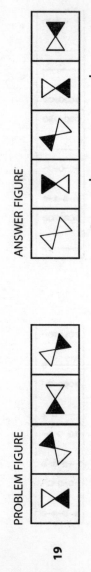

PROBLEM FIGURE

ANSWER FIGURE

a b c d e

19

PROBLEM FIGURE

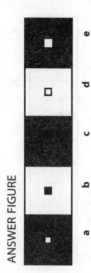

ANSWER FIGURE

20

ANSWER FIGURE

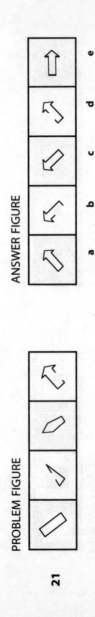

a   b   c   d   e

PROBLEM FIGURE

21

PROBLEM FIGURE

ANSWER FIGURE

a b c d e

22

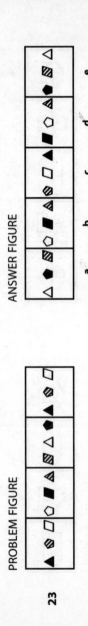

PROBLEM FIGURE

ANSWER FIGURE

23

PROBLEM FIGURE

ANSWER FIGURE

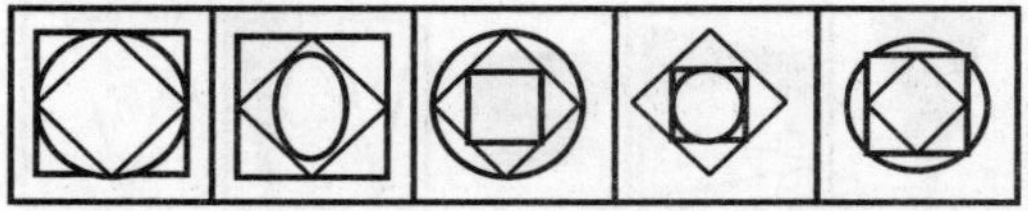

a   b   c   d   e

24

25

PROBLEM FIGURE

ANSWER FIGURE

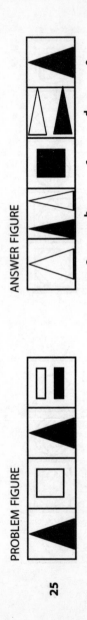

a   b   c   d   e

PROBLEM FIGURE

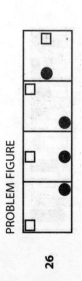

ANSWER FIGURE

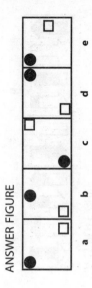

a   b   c   d   e

26

PROBLEM FIGURE

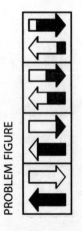

ANSWER FIGURE

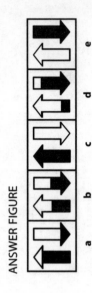

a   b   c   d   e

27

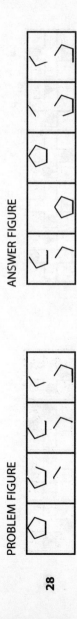

PROBLEM FIGURE

ANSWER FIGURE

a   b   c   d   e

28

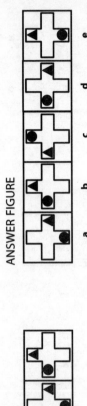

ANSWER FIGURE

a   b   c   d   e

PROBLEM FIGURE

29

48

ANSWER FIGURE

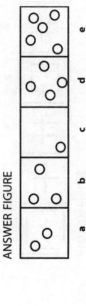

a   b   c   d   e

PROBLEM FIGURE

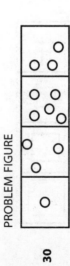

30

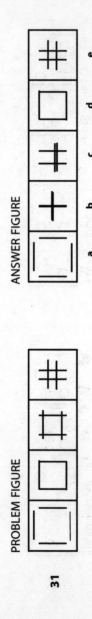

PROBLEM FIGURE

ANSWER FIGURE

a   b   c   d   e

31

PROBLEM FIGURE

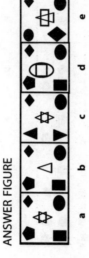

32

ANSWER FIGURE

a   b   c   d   e

ANSWER FIGURE

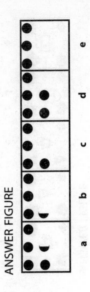

PROBLEM FIGURE

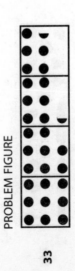

33

PROBLEM FIGURE

34

ANSWER FIGURE

a   b   c   d   e

ANSWER FIGURE

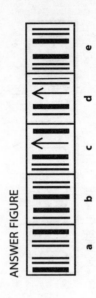

a   b   c   d   e

PROBLEM FIGURE

35

PROBLEM FIGURE

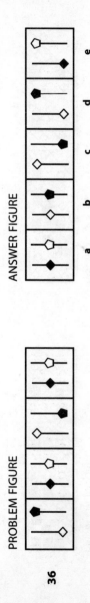

ANSWER FIGURE

36

ANSWER FIGURE

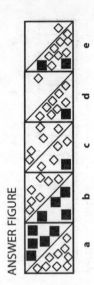

PROBLEM FIGURE

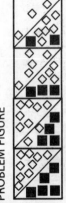

37

38

PROBLEM FIGURE

ANSWER FIGURE

a   b   c   d   e

ANSWER FIGURE

PROBLEM FIGURE

39

PROBLEM FIGURE

40

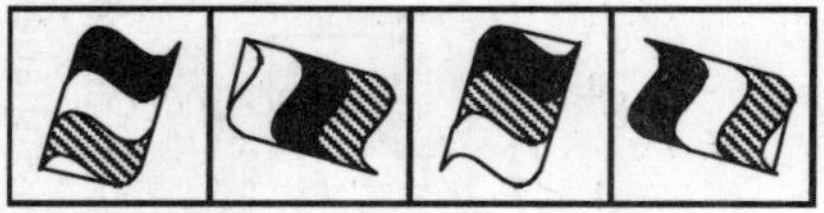

ANSWER FIGURE

a   b   c   d   e

TEST 2: OPP (RAVEN'S MATRICES) ITEM STYLE

(Answers to this test may be found on pages 138–150.)

This chapter exposes you to one of the classic item styles for diagrammatic/abstract reasoning. This item style simulates the Raven's Matrices, published by the fastest growing test publisher in the UK, Oxford Psychologists Press.

Study the examples. Then, when you are ready to begin, start the stopwatch or timer on your watch.

EXAMPLE 1

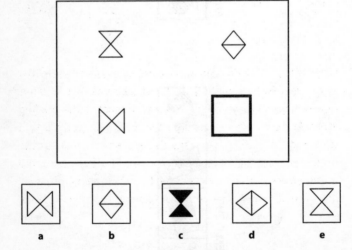

In the left column, the shape is an hourglass. On the lower part of the column, the hourglass shape rotates 90°. In the visible part of the right column, the shape has changed to a diamond. Therefore, in the missing part of the matrix, the diamond will rotate 90°. The correct option is therefore **Figure d**.

EXAMPLE 2

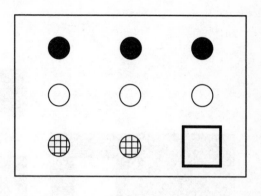

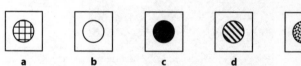

Each part of the matrix contains a circle. Going across each row in the matrix, the shading of the circle remains the same. However, going down each column in the matrix, the shading varies. At the top of each column, the circle is shaded black. In the middle of each column, the circle is white. Finally, at the bottom of each column, the circle has a grid pattern. Since the missing piece of the matrix is at the bottom of a column, it will therefore be a circle shaded with a grid pattern, as in **Figure a**.

TEST 2

You have 20 minutes to complete this test.

1

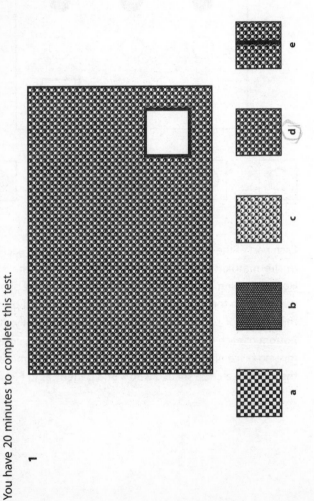

2

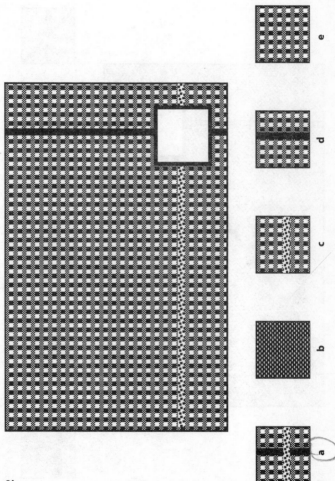

3

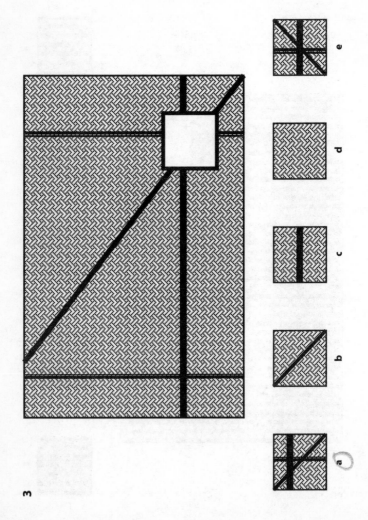

4

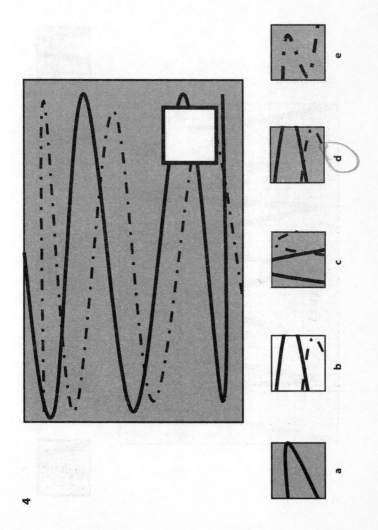

a   b   c   d   e

5

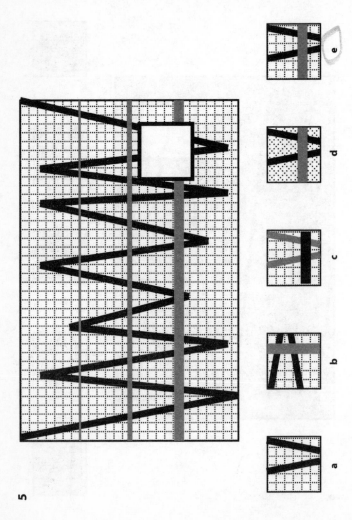

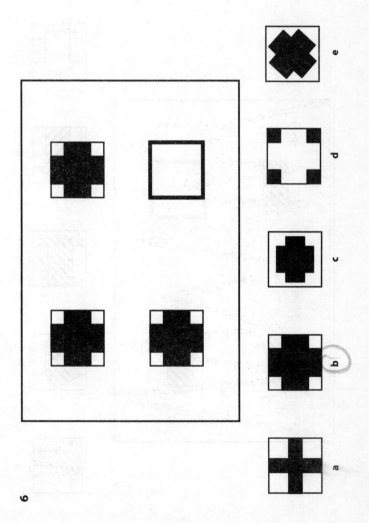

6

7

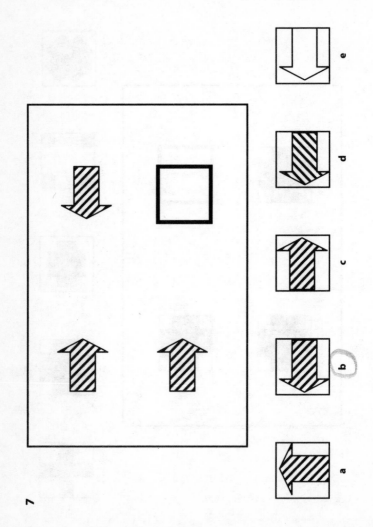

8

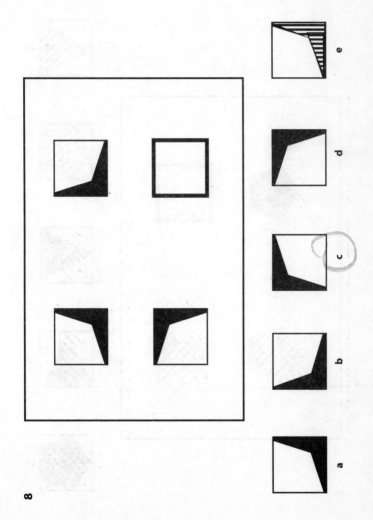

9

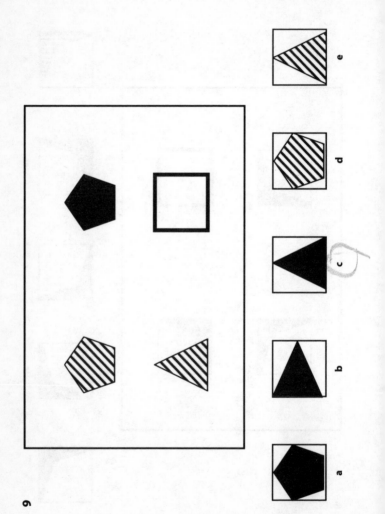

10

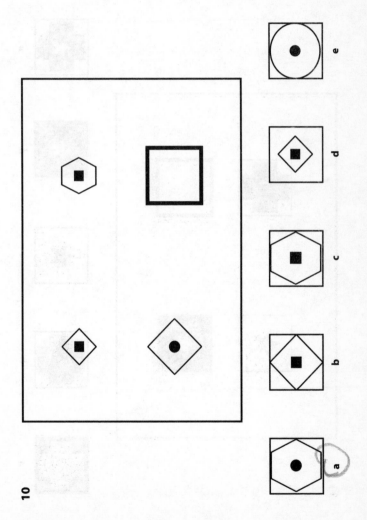

11

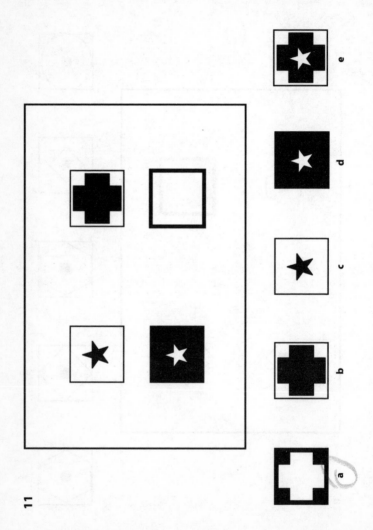

12

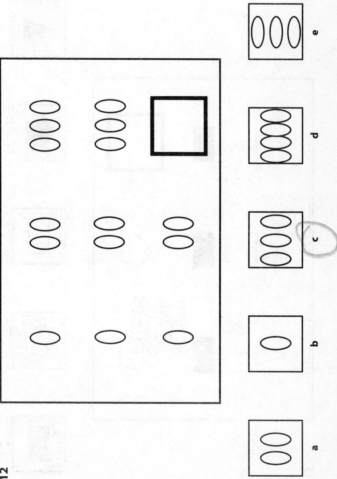

a   b   c   d   e

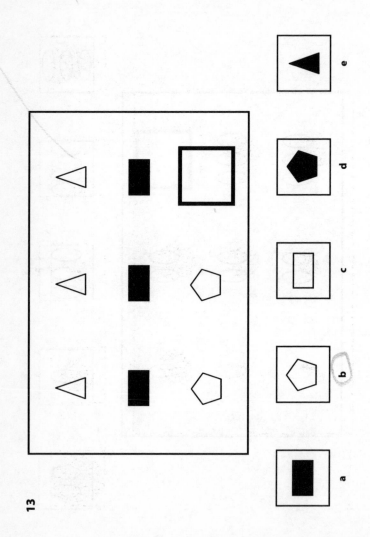

13

a b c d e

14

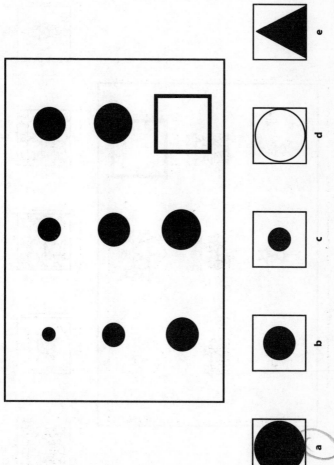

15

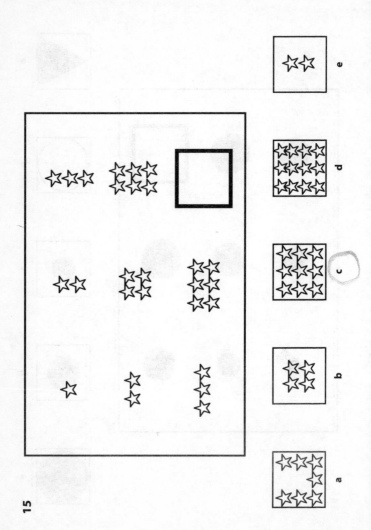

16

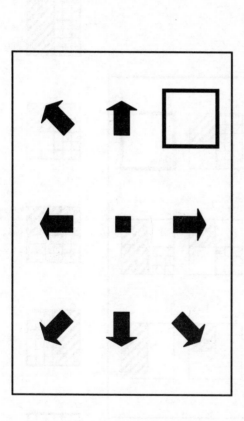

e

d

c

b

a

17

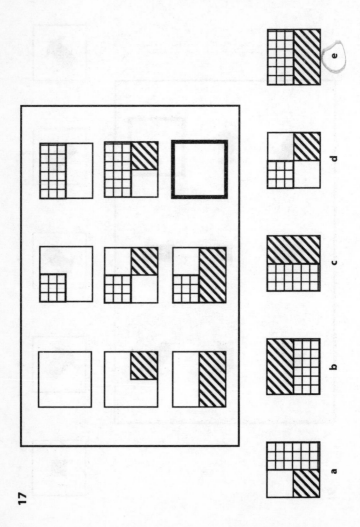

18

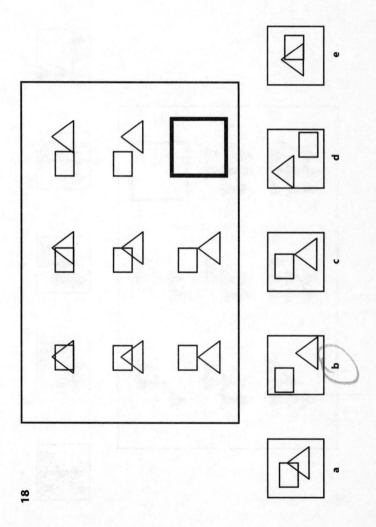

19

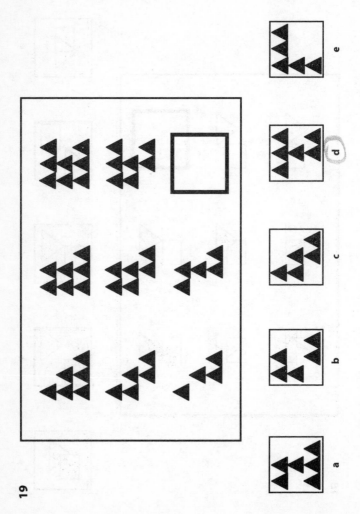

20

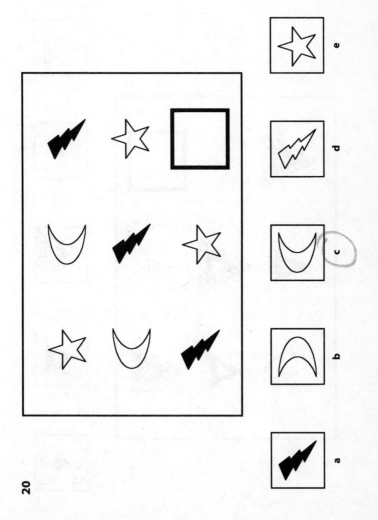

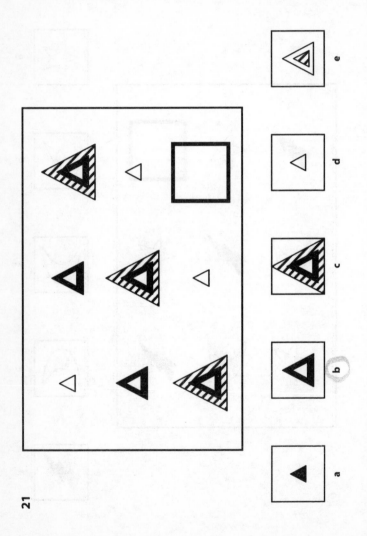

21

22

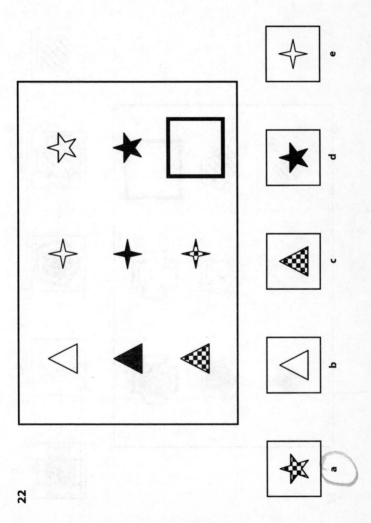

a   b   c   d   e

23

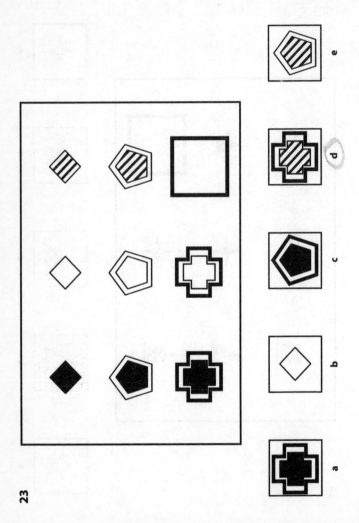

24

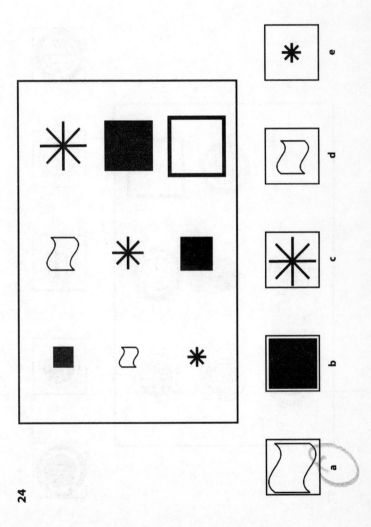

25

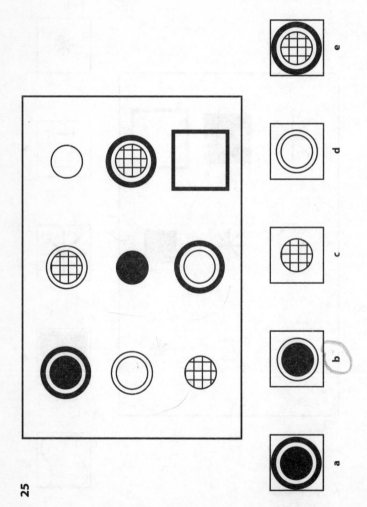

26

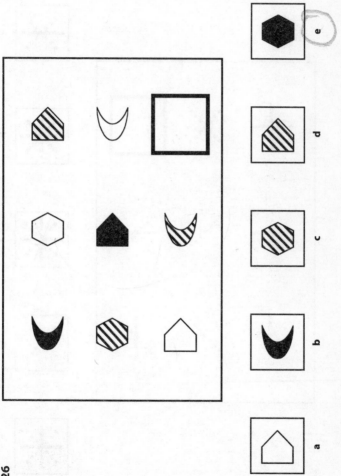

a

b

c

d

e

27

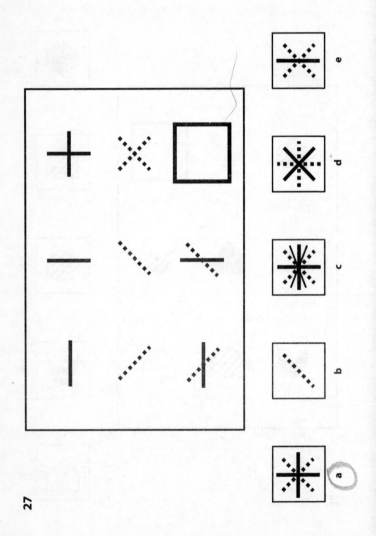

28

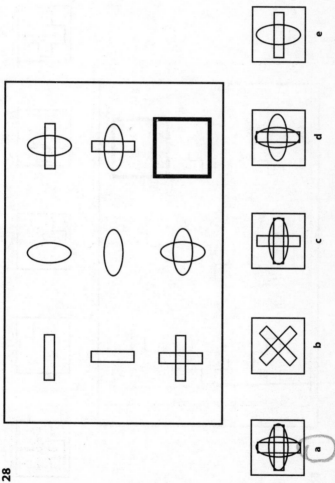

29

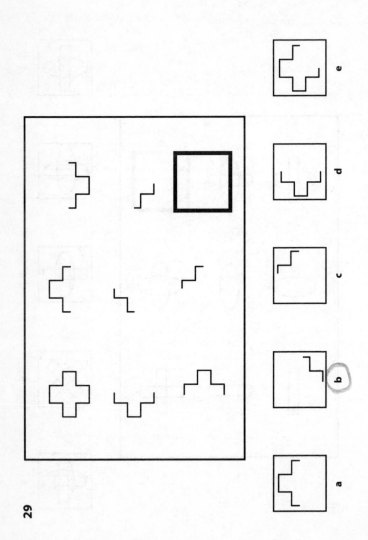

30

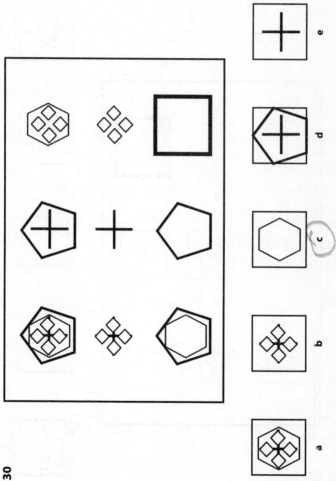

31

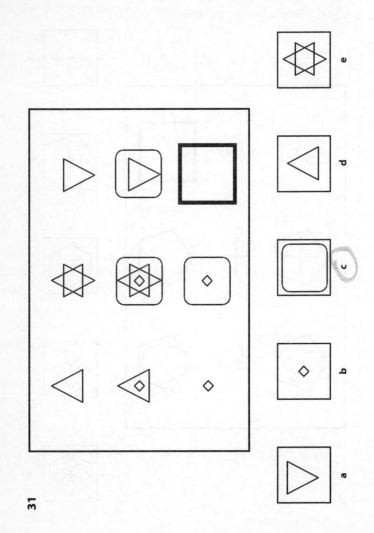

a   b   c   d   e

32

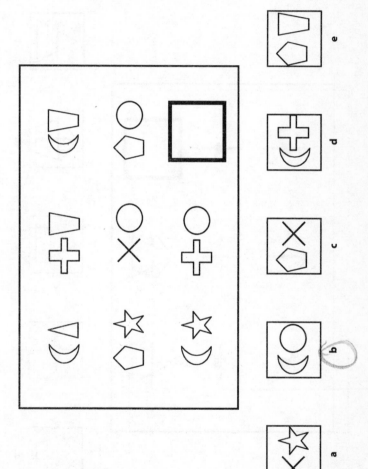

33

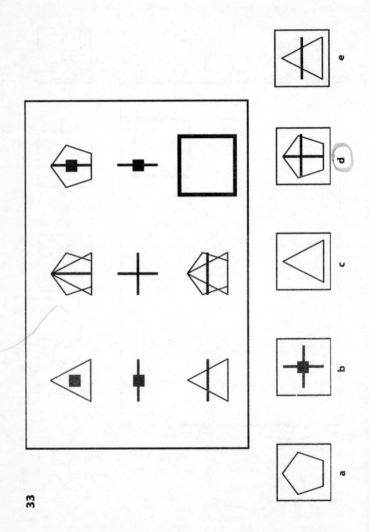

34

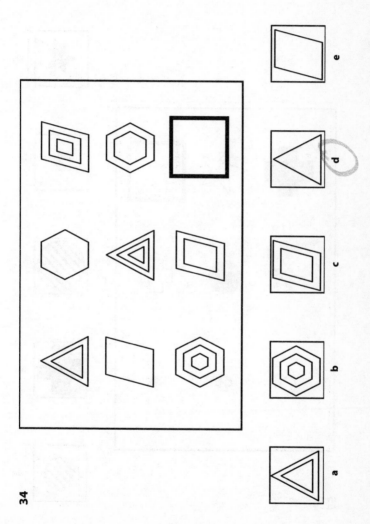

35

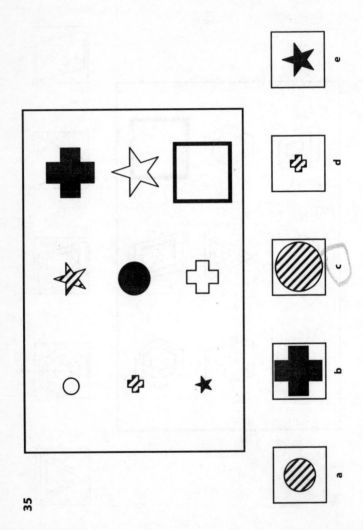

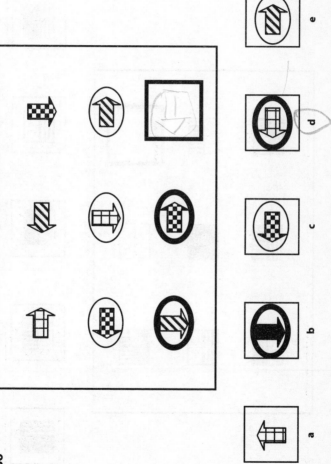

36

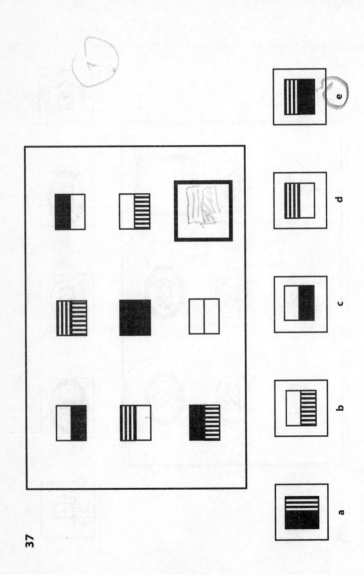

37

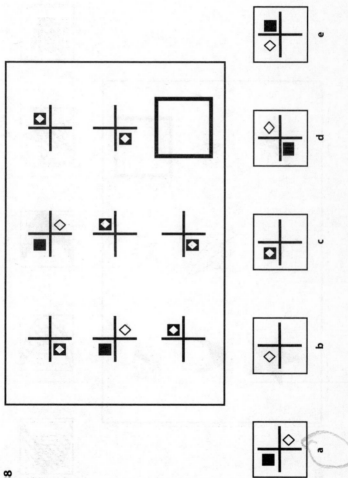

38

99

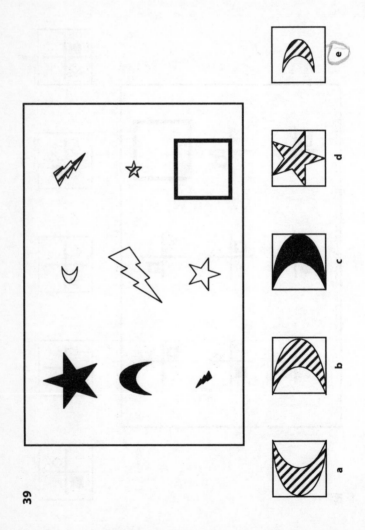

39

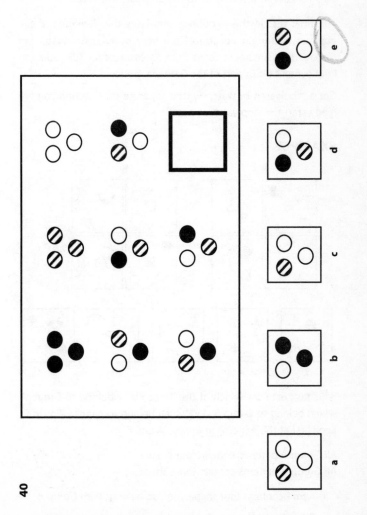

40

TEST 3: ASE ITEM STYLE

(Answers to this test may be found on pages 150–160.)

The final test in this sequence simulates the demands of the abstract reasoning portion of the very popular Graduate and Managerial Assessment series from Assessment for Selection and Employment (ASE), part of the Granada group.

Get a stopwatch or watch with a separate timer. When you are ready, start the stopwatch or watch.

EXAMPLE 1

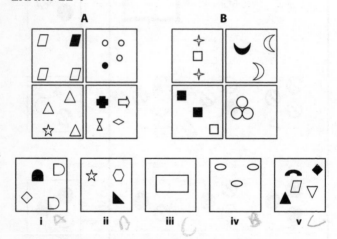

Your task is to say which of the items **i** to **v** belong to Group A, which belong to Group B, and which belong to neither (Group C). Look first at the patterns in Groups A and B.

All Group A patterns contain four shapes
All Group B patterns contain three shapes

- Item **i** contains four shapes, and so belongs with Group A.

- Items **ii** and **iv** contain three shapes, so both belong to Group B.

- As items **iii** and **v** contain *neither* three nor four shapes, they do not fit in with either Group A or Group B, and so belong to Group C.

EXAMPLE 2

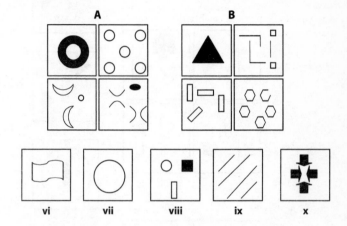

All Group A patterns are comprised of curved lines only
All Group B patterns are comprised of straight lines only

- Item **vii** consists of a circle, and so belongs with Group A.

- Items **ix** and **x** are made up of straight lines or straight-edged shapes, so both belong to Group B.

- As items **vi** and **viii** contain *both* curved and straight lines, they do not fit in with either Group A or Group B, and so belong to Group C.

TEST 3

You have 20 minutes to complete this test.

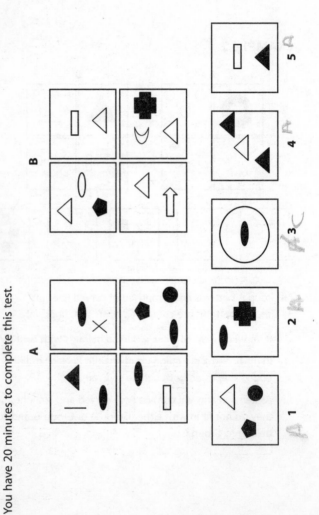

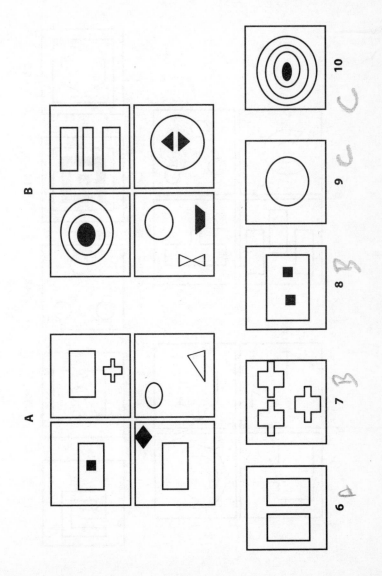

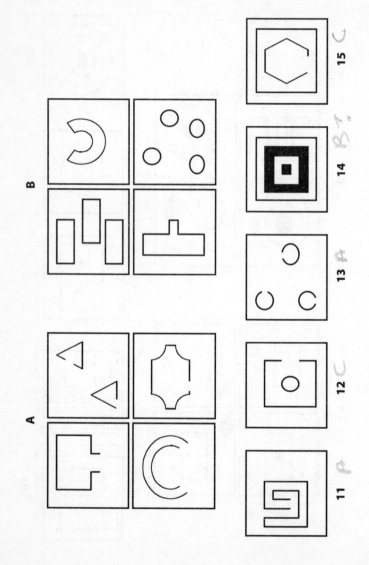

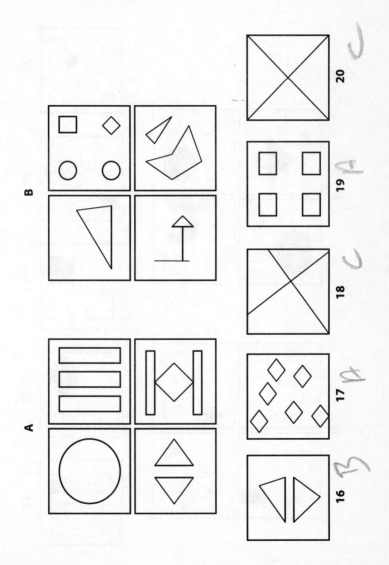

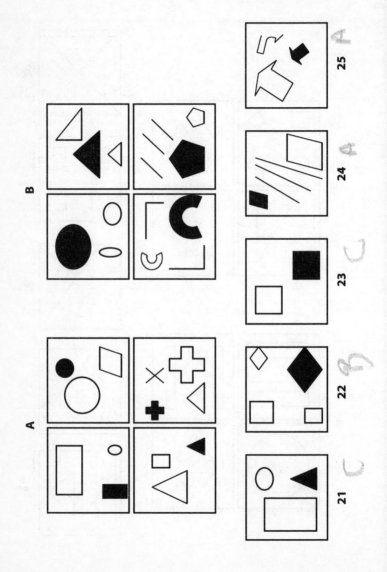

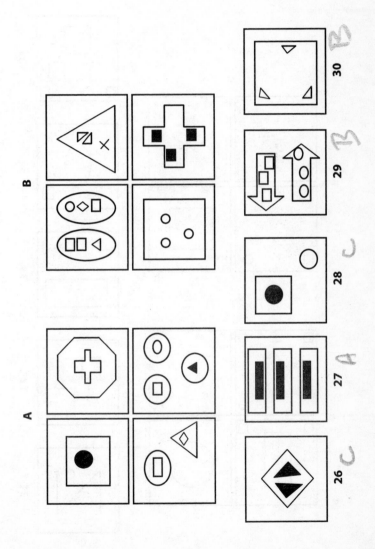

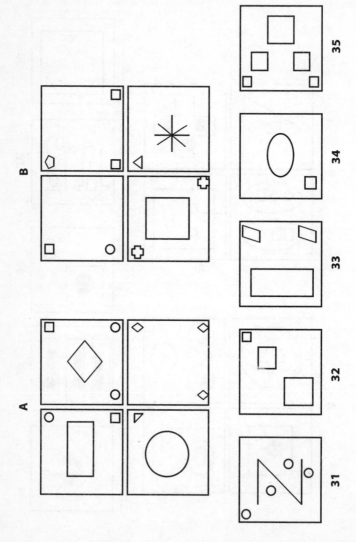

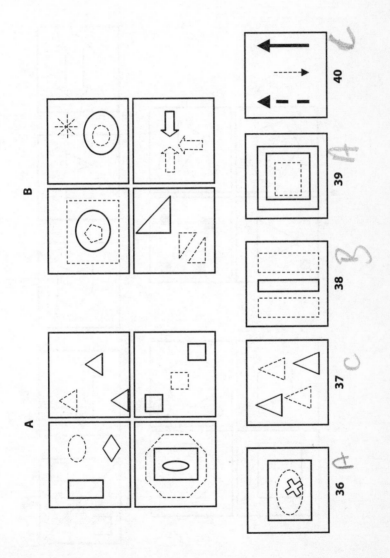

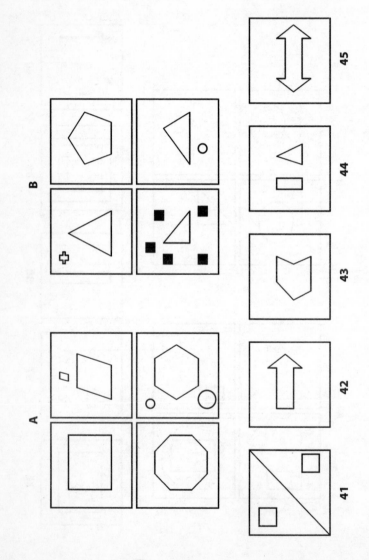

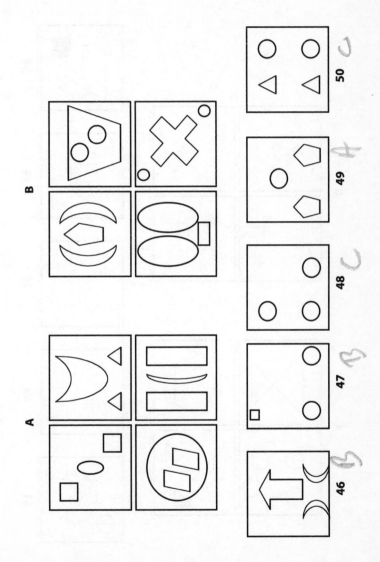

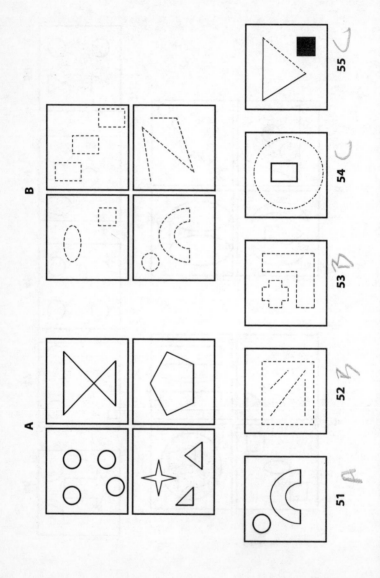

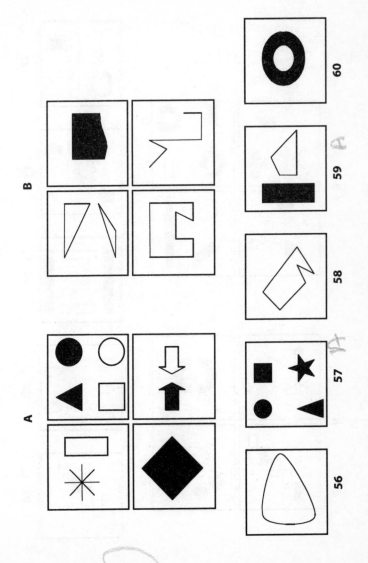

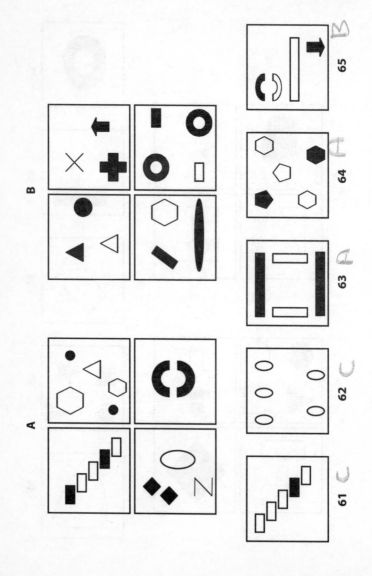

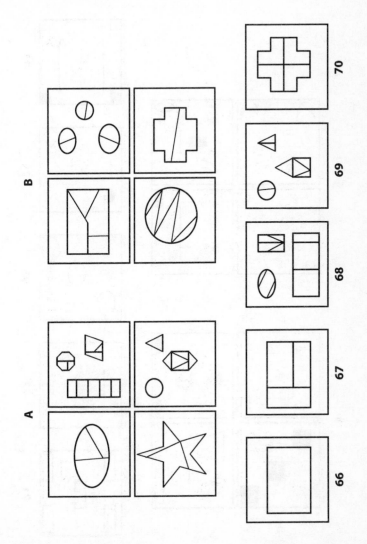

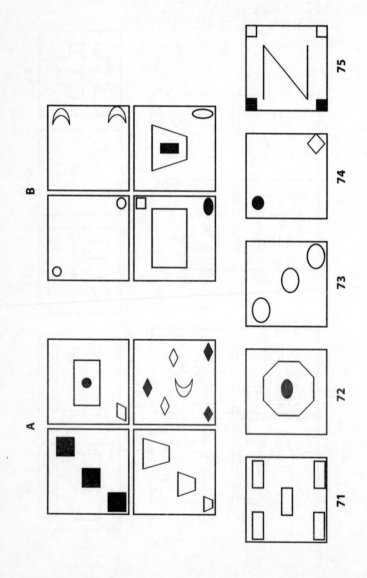

TEST 4: TOUGH ABSTRACT/ DIAGRAMMATIC QUESTIONS

(Answers to this test may be found on pages 160–162.)

Having gained some confidence and technique, you are now ready to attempt some much tougher questions.

Test publishers produce statistics in the test manuals on how difficult each question is, what are known as 'p' values. These indicate the probability that a question is answered correctly in a group.

The questions here all simulate questions which have very low 'p' values, i.e. where a very small proportion of people get the questions correct. So this test is a collection of tougher questions using the three item styles you have been using.

If you can do these, you are clearly ready to perform well on any abstract or diagrammatic test you are presented with, as you are unlikely to meet questions tougher than the ones you will be presented with here.

One general tip, useful for the first thirty questions (ASE style question) is always look first at the box with the least number of objects. All the other boxes must have a characteristic similar to this. This helps reduce the 'noise' and will allow you to identify quickly the basis of the relationship.

First you will be presented with ASE style items, then some SHL diagrammatic reasoning items and finally two Raven's Matrices.

Allow fifteen minutes for this exercise.

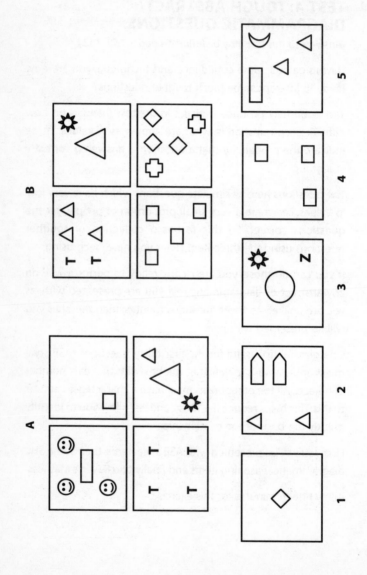

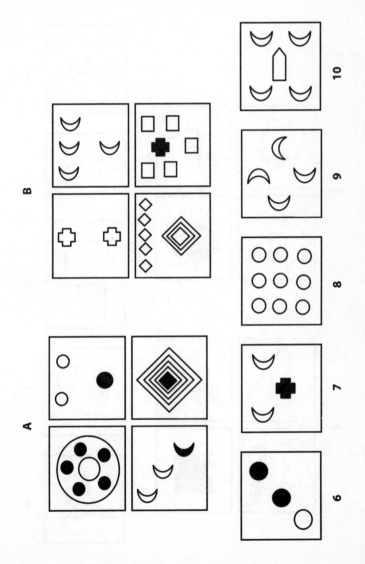

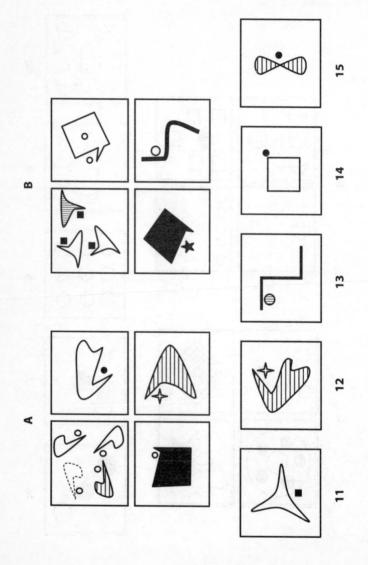

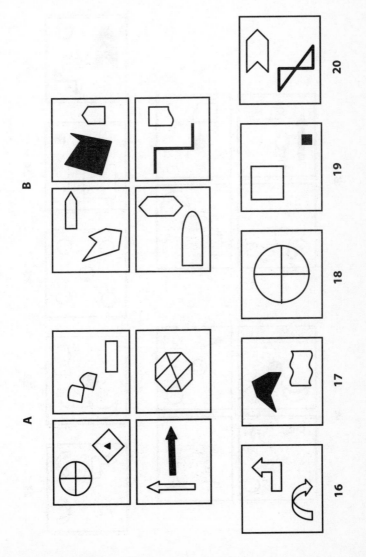

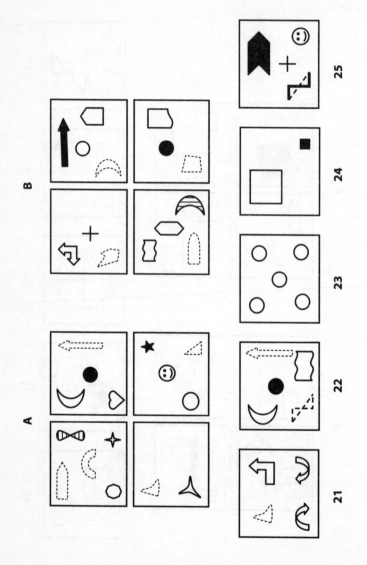

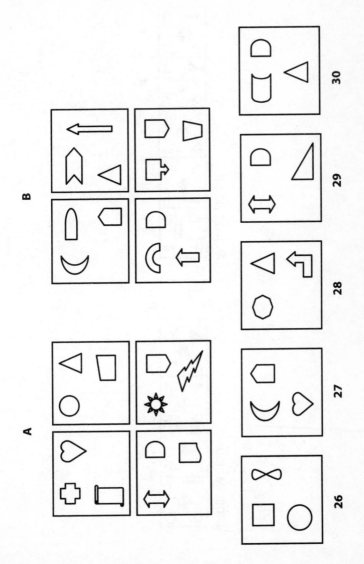

PROBLEM FIGURE

ANSWER FIGURE

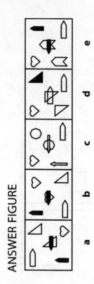

a   b   c   d   e

31

PROBLEM FIGURE

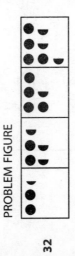

32

ANSWER FIGURE

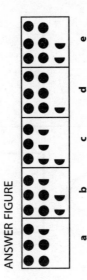

a   b   c   d   e

33

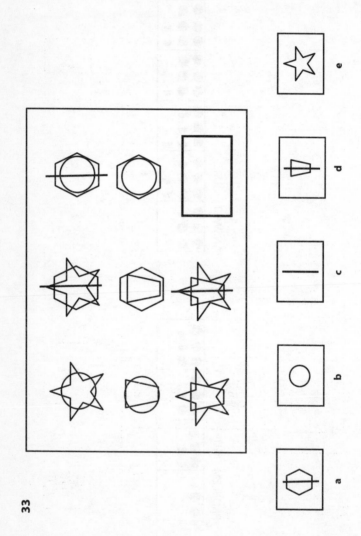

34

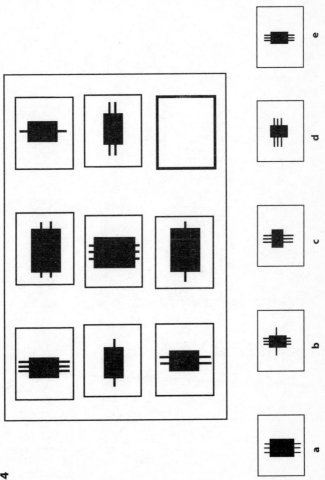

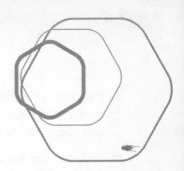

CHAPTER THREE
ANSWERS TO AND EXPLANATIONS OF TIMED TESTS

TEST 1: SHL/DAT ITEM STYLE

1 The shapes in the problem figures alternate between one square in the centre and two squares in a diagonal line. Therefore, the next figure in the series will have one square in the centre. As a result, the correct answer is **Figure b**.

2 A new square is added as an outline to the existing squares with each new problem figure. Hence the next (fifth) figure in the series will have five concentric squares, so the correct answer is **Figure a**.

3 The cross rotates 90° each time, so in the next figure in the series, the cross will have completed a 360° rotation and the black section of the cross will be pointing upward, as in **Figure c**.

4 The number of shapes comprising each new problem figure is one greater than the problem figure preceding it. As the final problem figure had five shapes, the next figure in the series would have six shapes. Therefore, the correct answer figure is **Figure d**.

5 With each new problem figure, one black square from the original check pattern becomes white. Therefore, the next figure in the series will only have one black square from the original pattern remaining in the bottom right corner. Hence, the correct answer here is **Figure e**.

6 One additional line is added to each new problem figure. As the fourth problem figure has four lines, the next figure in the series would have five lines, as in **Figure d**.

7 Each problem figure is comprised of a black square in the bottom left corner and a smaller white shape in the top right corner. With each new figure, the smaller white shape from the previous problem figure is superimposed upon the black square. As the final problem figure in the series has a white square in the top right corner, the next figure in the series would have a white square added to the shapes superimposed upon the black square, so the correct answer here is **Figure d**.

8 One point is removed from the star shape with each new problem figure. The removal of the points is in a clockwise direction. Therefore, the next figure in the series would have just the leftmost point of the star remaining. The correct answer is therefore **Figure c**.

9 The diamond shape in the problem figures is gradually elongated until it becomes a straight line, when it begins to return to its original shape. In the next figure in the series, it would have completely returned to its original shape and so the correct answer is **Figure c**.

10 The hourglass shape rotates 45° clockwise with each new problem figure and the shading of the hourglass alternates between black and white. Therefore, the next figure in the series will be white and a further 45° rotation will result in the shape appearing upright once more (**Figure c**).

11 Three lines are added to each new problem figure in a clockwise direction. So, for the next figure in the series, the addition of three lines will result in four batches of four lines. The correct answer is therefore **Figure b**.

12 Each problem figure has four shapes, so the correct answer figure is **Figure a**.

13 The problem figures alternate between a cross with a triangle and a triangle with a rectangle. As the last problem figure had a triangle and a rectangle, the next figure in the series would have a cross and a triangle, as in **Figure a**.

14 The number of shapes in each new problem figure is *increased* by one, while the number of sides of the shapes is *decreased* by one. As the final problem figure had four shapes with four sides, the next figure will have five shapes with three sides. Hence, the correct answer figure is **Figure e**.

15 With each new problem figure, an additional quarter of the rectangle is shaded in. In the next figure in the series, all four quarters of the rectangle will be shaded in, as in **Figure e**.

16 The large rectangle rotates 90° clockwise with each new problem figure and one of the rectangle's subsections is removed. Hence, in the next figure in the series, the remainder of the rectangle would be aligned horizontally and there would be just one subsection remaining. The correct answer is therefore **Figure b**.

17 The pattern of four shapes is rotated 90° anticlockwise each time. So, in the next figure in the series, the shapes will have completed a 360° rotation and so will appear in the same position as they did in the first problem figure. Hence, the correct answer figure is **Figure d**.

18 In each new problem figure, one black circle moves across from the line on the left to the line on the right. In the next figure in the series, all the black circles will have moved across to the right line, leaving the left line empty, so the correct answer is **Figure a**.

19 The hourglass shape rotates 45° clockwise with each new problem figure while the colour of each of the two triangular sections of the hourglass alternates between black and white. A further 45° rotation will result in the shape appearing upright, with the uppermost of the two triangular sections being black and the lower section being white, as in **Figure b**.

20 The central square in each problem figure becomes gradually smaller, while both the background and the central square alternate between being black and white. For the next figure in the series, the central square would become smaller than in the previous problem figure. The background would be black, while the central square would be white, hence the correct answer here is **Figure a**.

21 The shapes in the problem figures alternate between closed (complete) shapes tilting backward and open (incomplete) shapes tilting forwards. Hence, the next figure in the series will be a complete shape tilting backwards, as for **Figure c**.

22 The shape in each new problem figure is subdivided into a greater number of parts than the preceding problem figure. As the last problem figure had five sections, the next figure in the series would have six sections. Therefore, the correct answer figure is **Figure d**.

23 Each problem figure is comprised of three shapes – a triangle, a pentagon and a parallelogram, lined up horizontally. The line-up of the shapes rotates in the order triangle–pentagon–parallelogram. The shading of each shape also rotates in the order black–shaded–white. The next figure in the series would therefore comprise (from left to right) a white pentagon, a black parallelogram and a shaded triangle, as in **Figure b**.

24 Each problem figure is made up of three overlapping and concentric shapes – a square, a circle and a diamond. The order of the shapes rotates – diamond–square–circle. In the next figure in the series, the order will be square–circle–diamond, where the square is the largest shape, enclosing the other two. The correct answer figure is therefore **Figure a**.

25 The shapes in the problem figures alternate between a large black triangle and rectangles. As the last problem figure in the series involved rectangles, the next figure will have a large black triangle, as in **Figure e**.

26 The white square in each problem figure gradually moves clockwise around the figure, while the black circle moves anticlockwise. So, in the next figure in the series, the white square will be in the bottom right corner, while the black square will be in the top left corner. The correct answer figure is therefore **Figure a**.

27 The arrow pointing upwards in each problem figure gradually loses its black shading, while the arrow pointing downwards becomes progressively blacker. In the next figure in the series, the upward-pointing arrow will have become completely white, while the downward-pointing arrow will have become entirely black, as in **Figure e**.

28 One line from the pentagon is removed with each new problem figure and is positioned below the pentagon. In the next figure in the series, all but one line of the original pentagon will have been removed and repositioned below the original shape. Hence, the correct answer here is **Figure d**.

29 The black circle and black triangle are gradually moving around the cross shape – the black circle is moving in a clockwise direction, while the black square is moving in an anticlockwise direction. In the next figure in the series, the triangle will be on the leftmost point of the cross, while the circle will be on the upper point of the cross, as in **Figure c**.

30 In the second and third problem figures, two circles are added. However, on the fourth problem figure, this trend reverses and two circles are removed from the pattern. So, in the next figure in the series, a further two circles would be removed, leaving just one circle. The correct answer figure is therefore **Figure c**.

31 The four lines comprising each problem figure gradually move closer together. In the next figure in the series, the two horizontal lines and the two vertical lines will have effectively merged together, forming a cross shape. The correct answer here is therefore **Figure b**.

32 The problem figures have four black shapes in each corner. The outlines of the two shapes on the left are combined and form the centre of the subsequent problem figure. The two shapes on the right are moved across to the left hand side on the subsequent problem figure. So the next figure in the series will have two overlapping triangles in the centre and the two leftmost shapes will be a pentagon and a rectangle, as in **Figure a**.

33 The problem figures alternate between removing one circle and removing one and a half circles from the pattern. As one circle was removed for the last problem figure, the next figure in the series will have one and a half circles removed, leaving four whole circles remaining. The correct answer figure is therefore **Figure c**.

34 The bracket and brace shapes rotate 45° clockwise with each new problem figure and the shapes are inverted in alternate problem figures. In the next figure in the series, the shapes will have rotated 180° from their starting position and will not be inverted. The correct answer is therefore **Figure e**.

35 One arrow is replaced in each problem figure. Downward-pointing arrows are replaced by two fine lines, while upward-pointing arrows are replaced by one thick black line. As there was only one arrow remaining in the last problem figure, the next figure in the series will consist of two pairs of fine lines and two thick black lines, as in **Figure e**.

36 The diamond and the pentagon move up and down along the two lines. The shading of each of the two shapes alternates between black and white. In the next figure in the series, the diamond will be white and at the bottom of its line, while the pentagon will be black and at the top of its line. The correct answer figure is therefore **Figure d**.

37 With each new problem figure, one black square is removed and two white diamonds are moved across the diagonal line.

In the next figure in the series, there would be one black square remaining and all but one of the white diamond shapes would have been moved across the diagonal line. The correct answer is therefore **Figure d**.

38 The problem figures alternate between a circle with a crossbar and a scribble. In the next figure in the series, there will be a circle with a crossbar, as in **Figure b**.

39 In each of the problem figures, five of the nine stars are shaded black. Hence, the correct answer figure is **Figure a**.

40 The shape rotates 90° clockwise, while the shading of each of the subsections alternates between black, shaded and white. In the next figure in the series, the shape will be upright and the top section will be shaded, the middle section will be black and the bottom section will be white, as in **Figure c**.

TEST 2: OPP (RAVEN'S MATRICES) ITEM STYLE

1 The pattern consists of small black circles, arranged in closely set diagonal lines. The option, which would fit the missing piece of the pattern, is therefore **Figure d**.

2 The pattern is plaid, with a bold black line running vertically down the right side and a wide dotted line running horizontally along the lower part. As both lines appear to run through the missing piece of the pattern, the correct option is **Figure a**.

3 The pattern has a tiled effect, with a bold black line and fine black line running vertically down the right, a wide bold black line running horizontally along the lower part and a slightly finer black line cutting diagonally across the pattern. All three lines appear to cut across the missing piece of the pattern, hence the correct option here is **Figure a**.

4 The pattern consists of two overlapping curved lines – one solid black line and one dotted black line, zigzagging downwards on a grey background. The black line cuts across the missing piece of the pattern twice, while the dotted line curves off in a different direction. The correct option is therefore **Figure d**.

5 The pattern has a dotted grid background, with a bold black line zigzagging up and down from left to right. The pattern is cut across on three occasions by grey lines of increasing thickness. On the missing piece of the pattern, the thickest of the three grey lines cuts across horizontally, while one point of the black zigzag also falls into this space. The correct option for this question is therefore **Figure e**.

6 Each of the three visible parts of the matrix is a black cross shape outlined by a white square. So, the missing part of the matrix will also be a black cross in a white square. The correct option is therefore **Figure b**.

7 Both arrows in the left column are pointing right, while the arrow visible in the right column is pointing left. All arrow shapes are shaded with downward diagonal stripes. Hence, the correct option will have an arrow pointing left and will be shaded in the same manner as the other three arrows, as in **Figure b**.

8 On the top row, the pattern in the left square is a (horizontal) mirror image of the pattern in the right square, while in the left column, the pattern in the top square is a (vertical) mirror image of the pattern in the bottom square. The missing square in the matrix will therefore be a mirror image of either the bottom left and the top right squares. In addition, if all four squares were placed together, they would form a four-pointed star shape. Therefore, the correct option is **Figure c**.

9 In the left column, the shapes are both shaded with upward diagonal lines. In the shape visible in the right column, the shape is shaded black. On the top row, both shapes are pentagons, while in the shape visible on the bottom row is a triangle. So, in the missing piece of the matrix, the shape would be a triangle shaded black, as in **Figure c**.

10 In the left column, both shapes are diamonds, although the upper diamond is smaller than the lower diamond. In the visible part of the right column, the shape is a small hexagon. So, the shape in the missing part of the matrix will be a larger hexagon. Across the top row, both shapes have a small inset black square while, on the lower row, the visible shape has a small, inset black circle. So, in the missing portion of the matrix, the inset shape will be a black circle. The option which has a large hexagon with black circle inset is **Figure a**.

11 In the left column, both shapes are stars within a square. However, the shading of the shape inverts from a black star in a white square, to a white star in a black square. In the visible part of the right column, the shape is a large black cross in a white square. So, in the missing piece of the matrix, there will be a large white cross in a black square. The correct option is therefore **Figure a**.

12 The two leftmost columns in the matrix are identical to each other as are the two top rows. Therefore, to complete the third row and third column in such a way as to make them identical to the other rows and columns, three ovals, lined up horizontally are required. The correct answer is therefore **Figure c**.

13 Each of the top two rows in the matrix consist of identical shapes and the two leftmost columns are identical to each other. Therefore, the shape required to create a third identical column and complete the third row is a white pentagon, as in **Figure b**.

14 Going across the rows, the black circle is becoming gradually larger. Going down the columns, the black circle is also gradually increasing in size. Therefore, the missing piece of the matrix, on the bottom right, would contain a black circle which is larger than the circles immediately above and to the left. The correct option is therefore **Figure a**.

15 Going down each column, the number of columns of stars increases by one. For example, in the middle column, at the top, there is one column of stars, in the middle, there are two columns and at the bottom, there are three columns. Going across each row the number of rows of stars also increases by one – on the left, there is one row of stars, in the middle two rows and on the right, there are three rows. So, in the missing piece on the bottom right, there will be three rows and three columns of stars – nine stars in total. The correct option is therefore **Figure c**.

16 Going down each column, the arrow gradually changes from pointing upwards to pointing downwards – at the top, the arrow is pointing upwards, in the middle, the arrow is pointing out to the side (or is not pointing anywhere in the case of the middle column) and at the bottom, the arrow is pointing downwards. Going across each row, the arrow gradually changes in a similar manner from pointing towards the left to pointing towards the right. In the missing bottom right piece of the matrix, the correct shape would therefore be an arrow pointing toward the bottom right of the matrix, as with **Figure e**.

17 Going down each column, the lower half of the square is gradually shaded with diagonal lines – no portions are shaded at the top, in the middle the bottom right quarter is shaded and at the bottom the whole lower half is shaded. Going along each row, the top half of the square is shaded in a similar manner with gridlines. In the square at the bottom right part of the matrix therefore, the whole top half would be shaded with gridlines, while the whole bottom half would be shaded with diagonal lines. Therefore, the correct answer is **Figure e**.

18 The rectangle and triangle are gradually moving apart. The vertical distance between the two shapes becomes greater when moving down the columns, while the horizontal distance between the two becomes greater when moving across the rows. Hence, in the missing piece of the matrix, the two shapes will be completely separate from each other, with the rectangle diagonally above and to the left of the triangle, as in **Figure b**.

19 Each part of the matrix is made up of a pattern of black triangles. Going down each column, triangles are gradually *removed* from the left side of the pattern. Going along each row, triangles are gradually *added* to the top row of the pattern. In the missing, bottom right part of the matrix, two triangles will have been added to the top row of the pattern, while two triangles will have been removed from the left column of the pattern, as in **Figure d**.

20 Each column in the matrix contains a white star, a black lightning bolt and a white crescent shape. Each row in the matrix contains the same combination of shapes. No shapes are duplicated in any one row or column. Hence, the shape, which fits into the missing piece in the matrix, will be a white crescent shape. The correct option is therefore **Figure c**.

21 The premise is the same as for the previous question – three shapes are involved and each row and column in the matrix display each shape once. However, on this occasion the three shapes take the form of triangles of varying sizes, shading and number of layers. In the case of the bottom right portion of the matrix, the shape that fits will be a medium sized triangle, shaded black, with a smaller white triangle superimposed upon it. The correct option is therefore **Figure b**.

22 Going down each column, the shapes remain the same but the shading changes – at the top the shape is white, in the middle the shape is black and at the bottom the shape has a check pattern. Going along the rows, the shading remains the same, but the shape changes each time – on the left the shape is a triangle, in the middle the shape is a four-pointed star and on the right the shape is a five-pointed star. So, in the bottom right piece of the matrix, the shape will be a five-pointed star, shaded with a check pattern, as in **Figure a**.

23 Going down each column, the shading remains the same, but the shapes and the borders around each shape vary – at the top the shape is a diamond, in the middle the shape is a pentagon outlined with a fine border and at the bottom, the shape is a cross outlined with a bold border. Going across each row, the shapes and borders remain constant, but the shading varies – on the left the shape is black, in the middle the shape is white and on the right the shape is shaded with diagonal lines. Therefore, in the missing portion of the matrix, the correct shape will be a cross, outlined with a bold border and shaded with diagonal lines, as with **Figure d**.

24 Each column in the matrix contains a black square, an asterisk and a wavy rectangle shape. Each row in the matrix contains the same combination of shapes. No shapes are duplicated in any one row or column. However, going along each row from left to right, the size of the shapes also becomes gradually larger. Hence, the shape which fits into the missing piece in the matrix will be a large wavy rectangle shape. The correct option is therefore **Figure a**.

25 Each column in the matrix contains a black circle, a white circle and a circle shaded with a grid pattern. Each of the circles has either a fine border surrounding it, a bold border or no external border. The same combination of shading and borders applies to the rows of the matrix. No type of shading or border is duplicated in any one row or column and no combination of shading and border (e.g. white circle with a bold border; black circle with no border) is duplicated in the whole matrix. Therefore, the shape which fits in the bottom right section will be a black circle with a fine border. The correct answer here is therefore **Figure b**.

26 Each column and each row in the matrix contains a crescent, a hexagon and a pentagon. Similarly, each column and each row contains a black shape, a white shape and a shape shaded with diagonal lines. No type of shape or shading is duplicated in any one row or column and no combination of shape and shading (e.g. black crescent) is duplicated in the entire matrix. The correct shape for the missing portion of the matrix is therefore a black hexagon, as in **Figure e**.

27 The bottom part of each column in the matrix contains a combination of the top and middle shapes of the column superimposed upon each other. Similarly, the right part of each row contains a combination of the left and middle shapes of that row superimposed upon each other. Therefore, the shape in the bottom right corner of the matrix will be a combination of the two visible shapes in the bottom row of the matrix *or* the two visible shapes in the right column (both combinations will produce the same shape). The correct answer is therefore **Figure a**.

28 In the same manner as the previous question, the bottom part of each column in the matrix and the right part of each row contain a combination of the top and middle shapes of the column and the left and middle shapes of that row respectively. Therefore, the shape in the bottom right corner of the matrix will be a combination of the two visible shapes in the bottom row of the matrix *or* the two visible shapes in the right column. Hence the correct option here is **Figure a**.

29 The top part of each column in the matrix contains a combination of the middle and bottom shapes of the column joined to each other. Similarly, the left part of each row contains a combination of the middle and right shapes of that row joined to each other. So the shape in the bottom right corner of the matrix will be the shape which, when joined to the shape directly above will produce the shape at the top right of the matrix. (The solution could also be worked out by finding the shape which, when joined with the shape to the left of the missing piece, produces the shape at the bottom left of the matrix.) The correct answer is therefore **Figure b**.

30 As for the last question, the top part of each column and the left part of each row in the matrix contain a combination of the middle and bottom shapes of that column and the middle and right parts of that row. So the missing piece of the matrix will contain a shape which, when superimposed upon the shape immediately above it (or to its left) will produce the shape at the top right (or bottom left) of the matrix, i.e. **Figure c**.

31 The middle part of each column in the matrix contains a combination of the top and bottom shapes of the column superimposed upon each other. Similarly, the middle part of each row contains a combination of the left and right shapes of that row superimposed upon each other. As a result, the shape in the bottom right corner of the matrix will be the shape which, when joined to the shape on the top left of the matrix will produce the shape at the top middle of the matrix. (The answer could also be worked out by finding the shape which, when joined with the shape on the bottom left, produces the shape to the immediate left of the missing piece.) The correct answer is therefore **Figure c**.

32 Each part of the matrix consists of a pair of shapes. Going down each column, the shape on the left of each pair is the same at the top and the bottom of the column, while the shape on the right of each pair is the same at the bottom and in the middle of the column. Going across each row, the shape on the left of each pair is the same at the left and the right parts of the row, while the shape on the right of each pair is the same at the right and middle points of the row. So, at the bottom right part of the matrix, the shape on the left of the pair will be the same as in the pair at the top right (and bottom left) of the matrix – a crescent. The shape on the right of the pair will be the same as in the pair immediately above (and to the left) of the missing piece of the matrix. Hence, **Figure b** is the correct option.

33 The middle part of each column in the matrix contains a combination of the top and bottom shapes of the column superimposed upon each other. However, those features which are common to both the top and bottom shapes are not included in the middle part of the column. Similarly, the middle part of each row contains a combination of the left and right shapes of that row superimposed upon each other, with the exception of those features common to both the left and right parts of the row. So, the shape in the bottom right corner of the matrix will be the shape which, when joined to the shape on the top right of the matrix and after excluding the common features will produce the shape at the right middle of the matrix. (The answer could also be worked out by using the shapes across the bottom row.) The correct option here is therefore **Figure a**.

34 Each column and each row in the matrix contains a triangle, a hexagon and a parallelogram. Similarly, each column and each row contains a shape with one, two and no inset shapes. No type of shape or number of inset shapes is duplicated in any one row or column and no combination of shape and number of inset shapes is duplicated in the entire matrix. The correct shape for the bottom right of the matrix is therefore a single triangle, as in **Figure d**.

35 Each column and each row in the matrix contains a circle, a star and a cross. The shading of the shapes also varies, with a black shape, a white shape and a shape shaded with diagonal lines in each row and each column. As with previous questions, there is no duplication of any combination of shape and shading in the matrix. Going across each row from left to right, the size of the shape also gradually increases. The correct option for the bottom right part of the matrix will therefore be one which has a large circle shaded with diagonal lines, as in **Figure c**.

36 Each column and each row in the matrix contains an arrow pointing left, an arrow pointing right and an arrow pointing downward. The shading also varies with each row and column containing arrows shaded with diagonal lines, a grid pattern and a check pattern. Finally, the border around the arrows varies going down each column – at the top, there is no border, in the middle, there is a fine circular border and at the bottom, there is a bold circular border. So, in the bottom right portion of the matrix there will be an arrow pointing left, shaded in a grid pattern and with a bold circular border. The correct option is therefore **Figure d**.

37 Each part of the matrix is made up of a rectangle divided into two halves. The shading of each half varies independently of the other half. So, in each row and each column in the matrix, there will be a black top half, a white top half and a top half shaded with horizontal lines. Similarly, in each row and column there will be a black bottom half, a white bottom half and a bottom half shaded with vertical lines. There is no duplication of any combination of shading in the matrix. The correct option will therefore be a rectangle with a top half shaded with horizontal lines and a bottom half shaded black as with **Figure e**.

38 The black square and white diamond move partially around the cross independently of each other. On each column and each row, the black square moves in a clockwise direction from the bottom left of the cross, to the top left, to the top right, while the white diamond moves anticlockwise from the bottom left, to the bottom right, to the top right. Therefore, in the missing part of the matrix, the black square will be in the top left part of the cross, while the white diamond will be in the bottom right. The correct option is therefore **Figure a**.

39 Four parameters change in this matrix – shape, shading, size and orientation. Each column and each row in the matrix contains a crescent, a star and a lightning bolt shape. The size of the shapes varies, with a large, a medium and a small shape in each row and each column. As with previous questions, there is no duplication of any combination of shape and size in the matrix. Going across each row from left to right, the shading of the shape also changes, from black on the left, to white in the middle and shaded diagonally on the right. Finally, going down each column, the orientation of the shapes change – upright at the top, rotated 90° clockwise in the middle and rotated 180° clockwise (from the original, upright position) at the bottom. The correct option for the bottom right part of the matrix will therefore be one which has a large crescent, shaded with diagonal lines and rotated 180° clockwise, as in **Figure b**.

40 Each part of the matrix consists of three circles. The shading of each of the three circles varies (from black to white to diagonally shaded) independently of each other. No combination of shading is repeated in the matrix. Each row and each column in the matrix contains one black top left circle, a white top left circle and a shaded top left circle. The same applies to the top right circle – each row and column contains one black, one white and one shaded top right circle. For the bottom circle, the colour changes going across each row – on the left row the bottom circle is black, in the middle of the row the circle is shaded diagonally and on the right of the row, the circle is white. Hence, in the bottom right part of the matrix, the top left circle will be black, the top right circle will be shaded and the bottom circle will be white. The correct option is therefore **Figure e**.

TEST 3: ASE ITEM STYLE
ITEMS 1–5

- All Group A patterns contain a black oval
- All Group B patterns contain a white triangle

Therefore items 2 and 3 belong with Group A, items 1 and 4 belong with Group B, while item 5 does not fit in with either Group A or Group B, and so belongs to Group C.

ITEMS 6–10

- All Group A patterns are comprised of two shapes
- All Group B patterns are comprised of three shapes

Therefore item 6 belongs with Group A, items 7 and 8 belong with Group B, while items 9 and 10 do not fit in with either Group A or Group B, and so belong to Group C.

ITEMS 11–15

- All Group A patterns are comprised of open (incomplete) shapes

- All Group B patterns are comprised of closed (complete) shapes

Therefore, items 11 and 13 belong in Group A, item 14 belongs with Group B, while items 12 and 15 belong to Group C.

ITEMS 16–20

- All Group A patterns have at least one line of symmetry
- All Group B patterns are non-symmetrical

Therefore, items 19 and 20 belong with Group A, while items 16, 17 and 18 belong with Group B.

ITEMS 21–25

- All Group A patterns contain 2 similar shapes, the smaller of which is shaded black
- All Group B patterns contain 2 similar shapes, the larger of which is shaded black

Therefore, items 24 and 25 belong with Group A, item 22 belongs to Group B, while items 21 and 23 belong to Group C.

ITEMS 26–30

- All Group A patterns are comprised of larger shape(s) enclosing one smaller shape
- All Group B patterns are comprised of larger shape(s) enclosing three smaller shapes

Therefore item 27 belongs with Group A, items 29 and 30 belong with Group B, while items 26 and 28 belong to Group C.

ITEMS 31–35

- All Group A patterns contain a shape in the top right corner
- All Group B patterns contain a shape in the top left corner

Therefore, items 32 and 33 belong with Group A, items 31 and 35 belong with Group B, while item 34 belongs to Group C.

ITEMS 36–40

- All Group A patterns are comprised of 3 shapes, one of which has dotted lines
- All Group B patterns are comprised of 3 shapes, two of which have dotted lines

Therefore, items 36 and 39 belong with Group A, items 38 and 40 belong with Group B, while item 37 belongs to Group C.

ITEMS 41–45

- For all Group A patterns, the large central shape has an even number of sides
- For all Group B patterns, the large central shape has an odd number of sides

Therefore, items 43 and 45 belong with Group A, item 42 belongs with Group B, while items 41 and 44 belong to Group C.

ITEMS 46–50

- All Group A patterns are comprised of 2 identical straight-edged shapes and one curved shape

- All Group B patterns are comprised of 2 identical curved shapes and one straight-edged shape

Therefore item 49 belongs with Group A, items 46 and 47 belong with Group B, while items 48 and 50 belong to Group C.

ITEMS 51–55

- All Group A patterns are comprised of shapes with solid outlines
- All Group B patterns are comprised of shapes with dotted outlines

Therefore item 51 belongs with Group A, items 52 and 53 belong with Group B, while items 54 and 55 belong to Group C.

ITEMS 56–60

- All Group A patterns are comprised of shapes with at least one line of symmetry
- All Group B patterns are comprised of non-symmetrical shapes

Therefore items 57 and 60 belong with Group A, items 56 and 58 belong with Group B, while item 59 does not fit in with either Group A or Group B, and so belongs to Group C.

ITEMS 61–65

- All Group A patterns contain 2 identical black shapes
- All Group B patterns contain 2 different black shapes

Therefore item 63 belongs with Group A, items 64 and 65 belong with Group B, while items 61 and 62 belong in Group C.

ITEMS 66–70

- All shapes in Group A patterns are subdivided into an odd number of parts or are not subdivided
- All shapes in Group B patterns are subdivided into an even number of parts

Therefore, items 66 and 67 belong with Group A, 69 and 70 belong to Group B, while item 68 belongs in Group C as it has objects with odd and even subdivisions.

ITEMS 71–75

- All Group A patterns contain a 4-sided shape in the bottom-left corner
- All Group B patterns contain a curved shape in the bottom-right corner

Therefore, items 71 and 75 belong with Group A, item 73 belongs with Group B, while items 72 and 74 belong to Group C.

EXPLANATIONS FOR TEST 3 BY PARAMETER

One of the benefits of this book is it provides an opportunity to 'go backstage' and understand how questions were constructed. It is obviously useful to understand the options open to test constructors. Although questions seem complex, in reality the GMA style items are organised by just a few simple 'parameters' – aspects of the questions by which they are grouped. These include:

- Number
- Shape
- Position
- Size
- Symmetry
- Parity
- Closedness
- Lines

NUMBER

ITEMS 6–10

- All Group A patterns are comprised of two shapes
- All Group B patterns are comprised of three shapes

Therefore item 6 belongs with Group A, items 7 and 8 belong with Group B, while items 9 and 10 do not fit in with either Group A or Group B, and so belong to Group C.

ITEMS 26–30

- All Group A patterns are comprised of larger shape(s) enclosing one smaller shape
- All Group B patterns are comprised of larger shape(s) enclosing three smaller shapes

Therefore item 27 belongs with Group A, items 29 and 30 belong with Group B, while items 26 and 28 belong to Group C.

ITEMS 36–40

- All Group A patterns are comprised of 3 shapes, one of which has dotted lines
- All Group B patterns are comprised of 3 shapes, two of which have dotted lines

Therefore, items 36 and 39 belong with Group A, items 38 and 40 belong with Group B, while item 37 belongs to Group C.

ITEMS 41–45

- For all Group A patterns, the large central shape has an even number of sides
- For all Group B patterns, the large central shape has an odd number of sides

Therefore, items 43 and 45 belong with Group A, item 42 belongs with Group B, while items 41 and 44 belong to Group C.

ITEMS 66–70

- All shapes in Group A patterns are subdivided into an odd number of parts or are not subdivided
- All shapes in Group B patterns are subdivided into an even number of parts

Therefore, items 66 and 67 belong with Group A, items 69 and 70 belong to Group B, while item 68 belongs in Group C as it has objects with odd and even subdivisions.

SHAPE

ITEMS 1–5

- All Group A patterns contain a black oval
- All Group B patterns contain a white triangle

Therefore items 2 and 3 belong with Group A, items 1 and 4 belong with Group B, while item 5 does not fit in with either Group A or Group B, and so belongs to Group C.

ITEMS 46–50

- All Group A patterns are comprised of 2 identical straight-edged shapes and one curved shape
- All Group B patterns are comprised of 2 identical curved shapes and one straight-edged shape

Therefore item 49 belongs with Group A, items 46 and 47 belong with Group B, while items 48 and 50 belong to Group C.

POSITION

ITEMS 31–35

- All Group A patterns contain a shape in the top right corner
- All Group B patterns contain a shape in the top left corner

Therefore, items 32 and 33 belong with Group A, items 31 and 35 belong with Group B, while item 34 belongs to Group C.

ITEMS 71–75

- All Group A patterns contain a 4-sided shape in the bottom-left corner
- All Group B patterns contain a curved shape in the bottom-right corner

Therefore, items 71 and 75 belong with Group A, item 73 belongs with Group B, while items 72 and 74 belong to Group C.

SIZE

ITEMS 21–25

- All Group A patterns contain 2 similar shapes, the smaller of which is shaded black
- All Group B patterns contain 2 similar shapes, the larger of which is shaded black

Therefore, items 24 and 25 belong with Group A, item 22 belongs to Group B, while items 21 and 23 belong to Group C.

SYMMETRY

ITEMS 16–20

- All Group A patterns have at least one line of symmetry
- All Group B patterns are non-symmetrical

Therefore, items 19 and 20 belong with Group A, while items 16, 17 and 18 belong with Group B.

ITEMS 56–60

- All Group A patterns are comprised of shapes with at least one line of symmetry
- All Group B patterns are comprised of non-symmetrical shapes

Therefore items 57 and 60 belong with Group A, items 56 and 58 belong with Group B, while item 59 does not fit in with either Group A or Group B, and so belongs to Group C.

PARITY

ITEMS 61–65

- All Group A patterns contain 2 identical black shapes
- All Group B patterns contain 2 different black shapes

Therefore item 63 belongs with Group A, items 64 and 65 belong with Group B, while items 61 and 62 belong in Group C.

CLOSEDNESS

ITEMS 11–15

- All Group A patterns are comprised of open (incomplete) shapes
- All Group B patterns are comprised of closed (complete) shapes

Therefore, items 11 and 13 belong in Group A, item 14 belongs with Group B, while items 12 and 15 belong to Group C.

LINES

ITEMS 51–55

- All Group A patterns are comprised of shapes with solid outlines
- All Group B patterns are comprised of shapes with dotted outlines

Therefore item 51 belongs with Group A, items 52 and 53 belong with Group B, while items 54 and 55 belong to Group C.

TEST 4: TOUGH ABSTRACT/ DIAGRAMMATIC QUESTIONS

1 C; 2 A; 3 B; 4 A; 5 B

All Group A boxes have an object in the bottom left-hand corner. All Group B boxes have an object in the top right-hand corner and the middle, but nothing in bottom left-hand corner.

6 A; 7 A; 8 A; 9 B; 10 A

All Group A boxes have an odd number of objects in each box. All Group B boxes have an even number of objects.

11 C; 12 B; 13 A; 14 C; 15 C

If the larger Group A objects rotate anticlockwise they will cause the smaller Group A objects to rotate with them. Likewise if Group B objects rotate clockwise they will take the smaller Group B objects with them.

16 C; 17 C; 18 A; 19 A; 20 B

All objects in Group A boxes have four right angles each. All Group B objects have two right angles each.

21 A; 22 B; 23 A; 24 C; 25 C

All Group A boxes have a solid lined object in the bottom left-hand side. All Group B boxes have a dotted object in the bottom left-hand side.

26 C; 27 B; 28 A; 29 A; 30 B

All Group A boxes have one object which is symmetrical both horizontally and vertically; one object which is symmetrical either horizontally or vertically; and one not symmetrical at all. All Group B boxes have objects which are symmetrical either vertically or horizontally but not both.

31 e

The top left and bottom right symbols alternate every time. The bottom left symbol is always repeated in the centre. The top right symbol is always repeated in the centre but rotated anticlockwise through 90 degrees.

32 d

The are an even number of circles and odd numbers of semi-circles. The sequence is 2 circles and 1 semicircle, 2 circles and 3 semicircles, 4 circles and 1 semicircle, 4 circles and 3 semicircles. The next in the sequence is therefore 6 circles and 1 semicircle.

33 c

Moving horizontally across the top row, the symbols in the centre of the row (row 1, column 2), are composed of those symbols which are to be found in row 1, column 1 and row 1, column 3 (but not both). Similarly moving vertically down the first row, the symbols in the centre (row 2, column 1) are composed of those symbols found in row 1, column 1, and row 3, column 1 (but not in both). The only symbol that fits this pattern in row 3, column 3 is the vertical line. (You may also have noted that all the other symbols appear four times, except the vertical line which only appears three times – but this does not always apply to matrices, so beware of counting!)

34 e

Moving vertically, the central black box turns through 90 degrees. The black boxes are always intersected by one, two or three lines along the longest axis. The number of lines in each row or column always totals six.

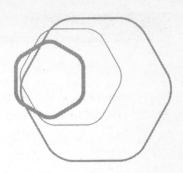

CHAPTER FOUR
DIAGNOSIS AND FURTHER READING

INTERPRETING YOUR SCORE

How did you get on? In psychometric tests, the raw score you achieved has little meaning. Performance is interpreted by comparing your score to a 'norm group'. This is a representative sample of some relevant comparison group. This might be the general population or more likely, in occupational test usage, it is a more restricted group such as 'senior managers' or 'first line supervisors'.

This book has attempted to provide you with experience of taking diagrammatic/abstract reasoning tests of different difficulty levels. Tests 1 and 2 simulate tests designed for use in the 'general population'. However, you may well still encounter them when applying for supervisory or managerial positions.

The third test simulates the abstract reasoning element of the Graduate and Managerial Assessment Series. As the title of the series suggests, it is designed for those applying for graduate level and managerial jobs. And if you found this test more difficult then this was intentional. The abstract reasoning test of the Graduate and Managerial Assessment series is one of the most intellectually demanding tests on the market.

The primary goal of this book is to increase your confidence, skills and thus score when taking a diagrammatic/abstract reasoning test. It is not intended to provide precise feedback on ability levels.

That said, here are tables which will enable you to make some sense of your performance.

TEST 1: SHL/DAT ITEM STYLE

Below Typical	0–17
Low Typical	18–21
Typical	22–28
High Typical	29–32
Above Typical	33+

Compared with A level students

TEST 2: OPP (RAVEN'S MATRICES) ITEM STYLE

Below Typical	0–28
Low Typical	29–31
Typical	32–34
High Typical	35–36
Above Typical	37+

Compared with a group of adults drawn from the general population

TEST 3: ASE ITEM STYLE

Below Typical	0–25
Low Typical	26–37
Typical	38–50
High Typical	51–64
Above Typical	65+

Compared with employed managerial staff attending training courses

TEST 4: TOUGH ABSTRACT/DIAGRAMMATIC QUESTIONS

Below Typical	0–8
Low Typical	9–13
Typical	14–19
High Typical	20–25
Above Typical	26+

Compared with employed managerial staff attending training courses

SUGGESTIONS FOR FURTHER IMPROVEMENT

MORE PRACTICE

If you have the time, have another go in two or three weeks. Leave it long enough for you to have forgotten the correct and incorrect responses to questions.

UNDERSTANDING AND MOTIVATION

Try to understand why you got questions wrong. Are there some question styles you find more problematic or parameters you find more difficult to manipulate?

One useful way of thinking about errors is to divide the task of answering a diagrammatic/abstract reasoning question into its two constituent elements. Diagrammatic/abstract reasoning tests involve:

Perception Many errors relate to simple carelessness in perception.

Analysis Errors can be the result of the failure to abstract 'item parameters' and synthesize the information this provides.

The perception element of diagrammatic/abstract reasoning tests involves 'seeing' the question. What is important here is both the attention to detail and the ability to see the whole. It means being sure of what you are seeing.

Analysis then involves analysing what is going on – making sense of what you are 'seeing'. This means being able to discern the parameters or concepts which are being used to arrange the item. It involves generating hypotheses about the important things to attend to in the question. The more difficult the question the more likely it is that more than one parameter is being manipulated at once.

Both involve being active, mentally energetic, being sure that your solution satisfies *all* of the available evidence in an item. This is clear from the evidence. High scorers try harder. High scorers tend to spend longer inspecting questions.

This suggests they are putting more effort into the task and testing more hypotheses about potential solutions to questions.

However, as suggested at the beginning of the text, speed is also important. So there is a compromise to be had between doing sufficient mental work on a question and not getting lodged in fruitless speculation.

Detailed studies of the strategies people use to solve diagrammatic/abstract reasoning tests suggest one of the main sources of error straddles both the perception and analysis elements of the task. These studies suggest errors stem from a simple unwillingness to devote sufficient mental energy to solve diagrammatic/abstract problems.

Interestingly, one of the other predictors of success on diagrammatic/abstract reasoning tests seems to be the extent to which individuals value intellectual as opposed to practical activity. Scores relate therefore not only to the effort and determination of individuals but also more generally to their values – the extent to which conceptualising is seen as a valued activity.

This brings us back to the first chapter of this book. It underlines the idea that your performance on a diagrammatic/abstract reasoning test is affected by a number of factors, many of which you have control over.

The fact you have purchased this book suggests you have already demonstrated the effort and determination to succeed which appears to be so important. In purchasing this book, you have also demonstrated an interest in conceptualising issues, another factor related to test performance.

These, combined with the familiarity which has come from practising all three major item styles, puts you in a strong position and ensures you are able to give of your best when the time comes to sit the test.

ON THE DAY

You must plan to arrive at the test centre in a state that is conducive to achieving your best possible score. This means being calm and focused. It is possible that you may feel nervous before the test, but you can help yourself by preparing in advance the practical details that will enable you to do well. Remember, it is unlikely that you are the only person who is feeling nervous; what is important is how you deal with your nerves! The following suggestions may help you to overcome unnecessary test-related anxiety.

1 Know where the test centre is located, and estimate how long it will take you to get there – plan your 'setting off time'. Now plan to leave 45 minutes before your setting off time to allow for travel delays. This way, you can be more or less certain that you will arrive at the test centre in good time. If, for any reason, you think you will miss the start of the session, call the administrator to ask for instructions.

2 Try to get a good night's sleep before the test. This is obvious advice and, realistically, it is not always possible, particularly if you are prone to nerves the night before a test. However, you can take some positive steps to help. Consider taking a hot bath before you go to bed, drinking herbal rather than caffeinated tea, and doing some exercise. Think back to what worked last time you took an exam and try to replicate the scenario.

3 The night before the test, organise everything that you need to take with you. This includes test instructions, directions, your identification, pens, erasers, possibly your calculator (with new batteries in it), reading glasses, and contact lenses.

4 Decide what you are going to wear and have your clothes ready the night before. Be prepared for the test centre to be unusually hot or cold, and dress in layers so that you can regulate the climate yourself. If your test will be preceded or followed by an interview, make sure you dress accordingly for the interview which is likely to be a more formal event than the test itself.

5 Eat breakfast! Even if you usually skip breakfast, you should consider that insufficient sugar levels affect your concentration and that a healthy breakfast might help you to concentrate, especially towards the end of the test when you are likely to be tired.

6 If you know that you have specific or exceptional requirements which will require preparation on the day, be sure to inform the test administrators in advance so that they can assist you as necessary. This may include wheelchair access, the availability of the test in Braille, or a facility for those with hearing difficulties. Similarly, if you are feeling unusually unwell on the day of the test, make sure that the test administrator is aware of it.

7 If, when you read the test instructions, there is something you don't understand, ask for clarification from the administrator. The time given to you to read the instructions may or may not be limited but, within the allowed time, you can usually ask questions. Don't assume that you have understood the instructions if, at first glance, they appear to be similar to the instructions for the practice tests.

8 Don't read through all the questions before you start. This simply wastes time. Start with Question 1 and work swiftly and methodically through each question in order. Unless you are taking a computerised test where the level of difficulty of the next question depends on you correctly answering the previous question (such as the GMAT or GRE), don't waste time on questions that you know require a lot of time. You can return to these questions at the end if you have time left over.

9 After you have taken the test, find out the mechanism for feedback, and approximately the number of days you will have to wait to find out your results. Ask whether there is scope for objective feedback on your performance for your future reference.

10 Celebrate that you have finished.

FURTHER SOURCES OF PRACTICE

In this final section, you will find a list of useful sources for all types of psychometric tests.

BOOKS

Bolles, Richard N., *What Color Is Your Parachute?* Berkeley, CA: Ten Speed Press, 2007.

Carter, P. and K. Russell, *Psychometric Testing: 1000 Ways to Assess Your Personality, Creativity, Intelligence and Lateral Thinking*. Chichester: John Wiley, 2001.

Jackson, Tom, *The Perfect Résumé*. New York: Broadway Books, 2004.

Kourdi, Jeremy, *Succeed at Psychometric Testing: Practice Tests for Verbal Reasoning Advanced*. London: Hodder Education, 2008.

Krannich, Ronald L. and Caryl Rae Krannich, *Network Your Way to Job and Career Success*. Manassa, VA: Impact Publications, 1989.

Nuga, Simbo, *Succeed at Psychometric Testing: Practice Tests for Verbal Reasoning Intermediate*. London: Hodder Education, 2008.

Rhodes, Peter, *Succeed at Psychometric Testing: Practice Tests for Critical Verbal Reasoning*. London: Hodder Education, 2008.

Vanson, Sally, *Succeed at Psychometric Testing: Practice Tests for Data Interpretation*. London: Hodder Education, 2008.

Walmsley, Bernice, *Succeed at Psychometric Testing: Practice Tests for Numerical Reasoning Advanced*. London: Hodder Education, 2008.

Walmsley, Bernice, *Succeed at Psychometric Testing: Practice Tests for Numerical Reasoning Intermediate*. London: Hodder Education, 2008.

Walmsley, Bernice, *Succeed at Psychometric Testing: Practice Tests for the National Police Selection Process*. London: Hodder Education, 2008.

TEST PUBLISHERS AND SUPPLIERS

ASE
Chiswick Centre
414 Chiswick High Road
London W4 5TF
telephone: 0208 996 3337
www.ase-solutions.co.uk

Hogrefe Ltd
Burgner House
4630 Kingsgate
Oxford Business Park South
Oxford OX4 2SU
telephone: 01865 402900
www.hogrefe.co.uk

Oxford Psychologists Press
Elsfield Hall
15–17 Elsfield Way
Oxford OX2 8EP
telephone: 01865 404500
www.opp.co.uk

Pearson
Assessment
Halley Court
Jordan Hill
Oxford OX2 8EJ
telephone: 01865 888188
www.pearson-uk.com

SHL
The Pavilion
1 Atwell Place
Thames Ditton
Surrey KT7 0SR
telephone: 0208 398 4170
www.shl.com

OTHER USEFUL WEBSITES

Websites are prone to change, but the following are correct at the time of going to press.

www.careerpsychologycentre.com

www.cipd.org.uk

www.deloitte.co.uk/index.asp

www.ets.org

www.freesat1prep.com

www.mensa.org.uk

www.morrisby.co.uk

www.newmonday.co.uk

www.oneclickhr.com

www.pgcareers.com/apply/how/recruitment.asp

www.psychtesting.org.uk

www.psychtests.com

www.publicjobs.gov.ie

www.puzz.com

www.testagency.co.uk

www.tests-direct.com

OTHER USEFUL ORGANISATIONS

American Psychological Association Testing and Assessment – www.apa.org/science/testing

Association of Recognised English Language Schools (ARELS) – www.englishuk.com

Australian Psychological Society – www.psychology.org.au

The Best Practice Club – www.bpclub.com

The British Psychological Society – www.bps.org.uk

Canadian Psychological Association – www.cpa.ca

The Chartered Institute of Marketing – www.cim.co.uk

The Chartered Institute of Personnel and Development – www.cipd.co.uk

The Chartered Management Institute – www.managers.org.uk

Psyconsult – www.psyconsult.co.uk

Singapore Psychological Society – www.singaporepsychologicalsociety.co.uk

Society for Industrial and Organisational Assessment (South Africa) (SIOPSA) – www.siposa.org.za